101 CYBER ANSWERS FOR LEADERS

How To Prioritize Risks, Manage Incidents And Enhance Your Leadership Impact Even Without Prior Cyber Experience

MARCO RYAN AND ANDREW FITZMAURICE

Pownall
Publishing

First edition

FREE
Bonus Content

Join our **VIP Review Panel** and get this detailed Cyber Incident Response Aide Memoire for FREE.

To download it:

- If you are on Kindle then click click the image above
- Otherwise simply use your phone to scan the QR code

SCAN ME!

CONTENTS

Introduction

In the summer of 2017, Soren Skou, the CEO of Maersk, the world's largest container shipping company, faced a crisis that would test his leadership and the resilience of his organization. On a seemingly ordinary Tuesday morning, Skou was informed that Maersk's computer systems were under attack. The company's screens went blank, and its operations ground to a halt. Unbeknownst to Skou and his team, Maersk had fallen victim to NotPetya, a devastating cyber attack designed to impact global companies and their supply chains. The attack crippled the company's international operations and caused losses to Maersk estimated at $300 million (Greenberg, 2018) and ultimately up to $10billion worldwide.

Skou found himself at the helm of a company in crisis. He quickly realized that the attack was not just an IT problem, but a threat to the entire business. With ships stranded at sea, containers piling up in ports, and customers growing increasingly frustrated, Skou knew his response would be critical.

In the following days and weeks, Skou and his team worked

tirelessly to restore Maersk's operations. They assembled a crisis team, bringing together experts from across the organization to assess the damage and develop a plan of action. Skou made the bold decision to rebuild Maersk's entire IT infrastructure from scratch, a process that would take weeks but ultimately ensure that the company's systems were secure and resilient.

Throughout the crisis, Skou was a visible and vocal presence, communicating openly with employees, customers, and stakeholders about the attack and the company's recovery efforts. He emphasized the importance of transparency and collaboration, recognizing that the company would need the support of its entire ecosystem to weather the storm.

As Maersk emerged from the crisis, Skou and his team recognized that cybersecurity could no longer be treated as an afterthought. They invested heavily in strengthening the company's cyber defenses, hiring top talent, and fostering a culture of security awareness across the organization. Skou's leadership during the NotPetya attack and subsequent focus on cyber security as a business enabler helped Maersk recover and emerge more robust and resilient.

The Maersk story powerfully reminds us of the critical role that non-technical leaders play in navigating the complex world of cybersecurity. By asking the right questions, understanding the business implications of cyber risk that stem from the answers to those questions, and taking decisive action to address them, leaders like Soren Skou can help their organizations overcome even the most severe crises and emerge stronger on the other side.

The Leadership Impact Series

"101 Cyber Answers For Leaders" is the second book in the Leadership Impact Series. The series consists of three books designed to work in conjunction. Book 1 is "Cyber for Executives Made Simple" and is a detailed guide for senior leaders and executives to understand the history, context, ethics, issues, and risks of cyber as it affects an organization. At the end of each chapter, the book provides the nine or ten critical questions an executive should feel comfortable asking to have the most impact in the boardroom or other meetings. In total, there are about 101 critical questions shared with the reader.

The second book—this one—is a companion to the more comprehensive first book. It takes those same 101 questions and answers them in detail. Each chapter has the context and information required to understand the questions and answers that give the book its title. This book is aimed more at managers and leaders of any seniority who wish to strengthen their cyber leadership impact.

The third book in the series, "51 Essential Cyber Terms Explained for Leaders," acts as a glossary on steroids and is designed to support both other books. Each of the 51 terms is formally defined, then explained simply and free of jargon, and then brought to life through a small case study.

Together, these three books help you understand the terms, context, appendices, risk, ethics, and strategies you need to succeed. They do so in simple, no-nonsense language and are supported by many real-life examples and case studies.

Although each book supports the other in the series, they can also be used as a standalone guide.

How to Use This Book

Throughout this book, we delve into the essential aspects of effective cyber security leadership, from understanding the actual cost of cyber incidents and developing proactive defense strategies to fostering cross-functional collaboration and leveraging cyber security as a competitive advantage. Each chapter explores a key topic and provides actionable insights and practical recommendations for leaders looking to enhance their organization's cyber security posture.

Each chapter is divided into two halves. The first half begins with an introduction and context to the topic that the questions are based on in sufficient detail to make the questions and answers in the second half of the chapter understandable. However, if you want a more detailed guide to the concepts, ideas, risks, strategies, and solutions of cyber security, then we suggest you buy the main book, "Cyber for Executives Made Simple."

The questions and answers we discuss in great detail in this book are a starting point for critical conversations and strategic decision-making, ensuring you and your team are well-equipped to tackle your business's cyber security challenges.

Whether you choose to read this book cover-to-cover or focus on specific chapters that address your most pressing concerns, "101 Cyber Answers for Leaders" is designed to be a valuable resource that you can return to time and again as you begin to increase your leadership within the ever-changing context of cyber security.

Throughout the book, the terms cyber security and cyber are used interchangeably. Indeed, in the UK the "security" part has been deliberately dropped to reinforce that the term is so much more than just a security issue. Similarly, whilst we talk about "cyber attacks" and "cyber threats," it is also correct to use "cyber-attacks" or "cyberattacks" and "cyber-threats" or "cyber threats." Because the terms are still new, neither Websters nor the Oxford English Dictionary have yet formally ruled which is the preferred of all the different nuances.

As you embark on this journey, remember that cyber security leadership is an ongoing learning, adaptation, and growth process. By arming yourself with the proper knowledge, tools, and mindset, you can lead your organization confidently through the challenges and opportunities that lie ahead, just as Soren Skou did during the NotPetya crisis. With "101 Cyber Answers For Leaders" as your guide, you'll be well-equipped to ask the right questions to ensure you lead with impact and drive meaningful change to secure your organization's future success.

Chapter 1

Unveiling Digital Threat Vectors

The internet has transformed how we live and work, serving as the foundation for global communication and driving innovation and economic growth. However, the digital world also presents hidden vulnerabilities - the constantly evolving cyber threat vectors and their persistent adversary, cyber crime.

Your company's data can be considered a highly prized fortress, containing financial records, customer information, and intellectual property---the core of your organization. Cyber criminals, the modern-day digital criminals, continuously search for methods to penetrate these digital barriers to steal, disrupt, or hold your data for ransom. As data is central to our personal and professional lives, comprehending the threats and developing a strong defense strategy is no longer optional; it's a vital investment for business leaders.

Demystifying Cyber

In this introductory chapter on cyber, we begin by providing a brief introduction to critical concepts. We explore the context of the increasing digital threat vectors and the significance of cyber. We then provide insights into essential terms and emerging threats, such as artificial intelligence (AI) and the Internet of Things (IoT). Finally, we offer practical knowledge to help you understand the cost of complacency and the advantages of a proactive cyber strategy.

Throughout this chapter, we will examine the structure of a cyber attack, clarify the terminology that often surrounds the topic, and discover how a proactive cyber strategy can provide your company with a competitive advantage.

The Anatomy of a Cyber Heist

A cyber attack can be compared to a meticulously planned heist. Criminals have a specific objective---stealing sensitive data, disrupting operations, or holding systems for ransom---and use various tactics to achieve it.

The entry point of a cyber attack is often a social engineering attack, where hackers exploit human psychology to gain access. Phishing emails, for example, may appear to be from legitimate sources, tricking employees into clicking malicious links or downloading infected attachments. Once inside, attackers may exploit software vulnerabilities to install malware, programs designed to steal data or spy on activities. In more sophisticated attacks, hackers might target the supply chain, compromising a seemingly unrelated vendor to gain access to your systems.

The impact of a successful attack can be devastating, with financial losses from data breaches and business disruptions potentially incapacitating an organization. Moreover, reputational damage can be severe, especially if customer data is compromised.

Deciphering the Cyber Buzzwords

The world of cyber is filled with technical jargon that can be overwhelming. However, don't worry! We cover key terms you will encounter to enhance your understanding of this critical business domain. If you want a more detailed glossary, simplified explanations, and an in-depth case study of that term, we recommend the "51 Essentials Cyber Terms Explained for Leaders" book.

- ***Phishing*** is a tactic that involves crafting emails to lure unsuspecting users into clicking on malicious links or attachments. These emails often appear from legitimate sources, such as your bank or a trusted colleague. Malware, on the other hand, is malicious software that can be installed on your computer or network without your knowledge, stealing data, spying on your activity, or even holding your systems hostage for ransom.

- ***Social engineering*** is another common tactic where hackers exploit human psychology to access information or systems. They may use scare tactics, flattery, or even impersonate someone you trust to trick you into divulging personal information or clicking on a malicious link.

- ***Botnets*** are networks of devices infected with malicious software controlled remotely by a hacker, typically without the device owners' knowledge. Botnets are commonly used to send spam emails or carry out Distributed Denial-of-Service (DDoS) attacks, where multiple DoS attacks are launched from various locations, flooding a website or server with traffic to make it inaccessible to legitimate users.

- ***Zero-day attacks*** are particularly dangerous as they exploit software vulnerabilities that the vendor is unaware of. The term "zero day" refers to the fact that the developers have had zero days to address and patch the vulnerability. This means that the attack occurs on the same day that the vulnerability is discovered, taking advantage of the security hole before a fix becomes available.

- ***Encryption*** is the process of scrambling data so that it can only be read by someone with the decryption key, making it essential for protecting sensitive data. Firewalls, security systems that monitor incoming and outgoing network traffic and block malicious activity, are another crucial component of cyber.

- ***Artificial Intelligence (AI)***, a branch of computer science dealing with creating intelligent agents that can reason, learn, and act autonomously, has the potential to revolutionize many aspects of our lives. However, it also poses new security challenges that we must address. For example, a Hong Kong bank was defrauded of HK$200 Million when scammers orchestrated a fake video conference call using deep-fake technology to impersonate multiple company executives, ultimately convincing an employee to transfer a substantial sum of HK$200 million.

AI in a Cyber Context: Friend or Foe?

AI has emerged as a potential double-edged sword in cyber, with beneficial and malicious applications.

Cyber criminals increasingly use AI to automate attacks, making them more sophisticated and challenging to detect. AI can identify software vulnerabilities, personalize phishing attacks, and even automate the launching of cyber attacks. This AI-powered approach to cyber crime poses a significant challenge for cyber professionals.

Fortunately, AI can also be a powerful tool for defending against cyber attacks. AI-powered security systems can analyze vast amounts of data to identify patterns and anomalies that might indicate a cyber attack in progress. Machine learning algorithms can constantly learn and adapt to new threats, providing a more robust defense than traditional rule-based systems.

The key takeaway is that AI is not inherently good or bad for cyber; it's the application of AI that matters. As we continue to develop and deploy AI systems, it's crucial to prioritize security and ensure that these technologies are used responsibly. But AI does not operate in isolation. Indeed, the ability of AI algorithms to be deployed on the smallest and most remote sensors and run right at the "edge" of the network of connected things (IoT) makes it, in cyber terms, such a prominent threat vector.

The Internet of Things (IoT): Expanding the Attack Surface

The Internet of Things (IoT) refers to the ever-growing network of physical devices connected to the Internet, capable of collecting and sharing data. The IoT is rapidly transforming our world, from smart thermostats to connected cars. However, this interconnectedness also creates new vulnerabilities that cyber criminals can exploit.

With millions of devices, each potentially harboring security weaknesses, connected to a vast network, hackers could exploit these vulnerabilities to launch large-scale attacks, disrupt critical infrastructure, or steal sensitive data.

One significant concern is the lack of standardized security protocols for IoT devices, making it challenging to ensure that all devices on a network are adequately secured. Additionally, many businesses still rely on legacy systems that may not have been designed with security in mind. These systems can be particularly vulnerable to cyber attacks when connected to IoT devices.

For example, Norwegian firm Norsk Hydro suffered a ransomware attack that affected its operations across Europe and the U.S. The attackers likely exploited vulnerabilities in the company's IoT devices as part of their entry strategy. The impact was significant, halting production in several plants and forcing some of the company's units to switch to manual operations. The financial impact was estimated to be in the tens of millions of dollars. Another example is the Verkada Camera Hack in March 2021, when a group of hackers gained access to the internal networks of Verkada, a company specializing in cloud-based security cameras used across industries. They breached the system by exploiting a super admin account, accessing camera feeds from 150,000 surveillance cameras installed in hospitals, companies, police departments, prisons, and schools. This breach highlighted the risks of connected devices and the potential for widespread surveillance and privacy violations.

Investing in robust cyber measures is crucial for any business looking to leverage the power of the IoT. This includes prioritizing security in designing and developing IoT devices, implementing strong authentication and encryption protocols, and regularly updating and patching devices to address newly discovered vulnerabilities.

Building a Proactive Cyber Strategy: Your Competitive Edge

Now that we've explored the threats and emerging technologies let's focus on building a proactive cyber strategy.

The first step is to conduct a comprehensive security risk assessment to identify your company's most valuable assets and potential vulnerabilities. This assessment will help you prioritize your security efforts and allocate resources effectively.

Next, a clear security policy that outlines acceptable use of company technology and data access procedures should be developed. This policy should be regularly reviewed and updated to remain relevant and practical.

Investing in employee training is another critical component of a proactive cyber strategy. Educate your employees about cyber best practices, including identifying phishing emails and avoiding social engineering attacks. Regular training sessions can help foster a culture of cyber awareness within your organization.

Implementing robust security measures, such as firewalls, anti-virus software, and other security tools, is essential to protect your network and devices from potential threats. Additionally, developing an incident response plan that outlines how to respond to a cyber attack, contain the damage, and recover your data can help minimize the impact of a security breach.

Finally, staying informed about the latest cyber threats and vulnerabilities is crucial for maintaining a strong cyber posture. Regularly monitoring cyber news, attending industry events, and participating in information-sharing initiatives can help you stay ahead of emerging threats.

By taking a proactive approach to cyber, you can make your business more resilient to cyber attacks and demonstrate to clients and partners that you take data security seriously. This, in turn, can give you a competitive edge in an increasingly digital business landscape.

Answers To Key Questions

Question 1: What cyber attacks pose the greatest threat to our industry, and how are we prepared to counter them?

Answer: The specific cyber threats facing your industry will vary depending on the type of data you handle. Financial institutions, for example, are prime targets for data breaches that steal financial information or disrupt critical transactions. Healthcare providers hold sensitive patient data, making them targets for attacks that aim to steal this information or lock healthcare providers out of their systems. Retailers collect customer data, including credit card information, making them targets for data breaches and attacks that disrupt sales through point-of-sale systems.

Understanding the threats specific to your industry is the first step in developing an effective defense strategy. Once you know what threats you face, work with your cyber team to implement regular employee training on identifying phishing emails and other social engineering attacks, keep all software up-to-date with the latest security patches, and develop an incident response plan to minimize damage and downtime in the event of a cyber attack.

Question 2: How do we simplify cyber jargon for better communication across all departments?

Answer: Effective communication is critical to building a strong cyber culture within your organization. Develop a cyber glossary that defines key terms in plain language, or consider resources like the "51 Essential Cyber Terms Explained for Leaders" book, which provides descriptions, explanations, and real-life case studies to help you better understand the subject.

Encourage plain language communication when discussing cyber issues, focusing on explaining concepts in a way everyone can understand. Invest in regular cyber awareness training sessions to help employees understand common threats and how to protect themselves and the company from cyber attacks.

Question 3: In what ways are emerging technologies like AI and IoT creating new vulnerabilities, and how are we addressing them?

Answer: Artificial Intelligence (AI) and the Internet of Things (IoT) are transforming our world, but they also introduce new security challenges. Cyber criminals can use AI to automate tasks and launch more sophisticated attacks, such as personalizing phishing emails or identifying software vulnerabilities. IoT devices often have weak security protocols, making them vulnerable to hacks that can be exploited to launch large-scale attacks or steal sensitive data.

To address these emerging threats, focus on secure coding practices for AI development, using secure coding practices and carefully vetting any third-party code. For IoT devices, prioritize robust security features, such as encryption and the ability to receive security updates, and segment IoT devices on a separate network to minimize potential damage from a security breach.

Question 4: Can we quantify the financial impact of not investing adequately in cyber?

Answer: The financial costs of a cyber attack can be significant, including data breach fines imposed by regulatory bodies, legal fees incurred from lawsuits, lost revenue and productivity due to business disruption, and reputational damage that can make attracting and retaining customers difficult.

For example, the Equifax data breach in 2017 exposed the personal information of 147 million people. The company faced numerous lawsuits, regulatory fines, and a settlement of up to $700 million. The breach also significantly impacted Equifax's reputation, with many customers losing trust in its ability to protect their sensitive data.

In May 2021, Colonial Pipeline, the most extensive fuel pipeline system in the United States, fell victim to a ransomware attack. The attackers, believed to be an Eastern European hacking group called DarkSide, infiltrated Colonial Pipeline's network and encrypted their data, demanding a ransom payment in exchange for the decryption key. The attack forced Colonial Pipeline to shut down its entire pipeline network, which spans over 5,500 miles and carries nearly half of the East Coast's fuel supplies. The disruption led to widespread gasoline shortages, panic buying, and a surge in gas prices across the southeastern United States. Colonial Pipeline ultimately paid the attackers a ransom of $4.4 million in Bitcoin to restore their systems. However, the total cost of the attack is estimated to be much higher. The final costs have not yet been calculated but are already reaching hundreds of millions of dollars when considering the revenue loss, recovery efforts, and damage to the company's reputation.

These examples demonstrate the potential financial impact of not investing adequately in cyber. The cost of a cyber attack can easily outweigh the cost of implementing cyber measures. By investing in cyber, you can protect your organization from financial losses and reputational damage.

Question 5: How can we incentivize employees to prioritize cyber best practices?

Answer: Strong leadership commitment to cyber also plays a vital role in setting the tone for the entire organization. When leaders actively participate in security awareness campaigns, discuss the importance of cyber during meetings, and lead by example by following best practices themselves, it reinforces the message that cyber is a top priority. Instead of solely focusing on punishments for security breaches, emphasizing positive reinforcement and highlighting the positive outcomes of good security practices can be more effective. Sharing success stories of how employee vigilance prevented a potential breach or how following best practices helped protect sensitive data can encourage others to follow suit.

Creating a culture of cyber awareness within your organization is crucial. Implementing recognition programs that reward employees who demonstrate exemplary cyber practices, such as reporting suspicious emails or completing security training on time, can be a powerful motivator. These rewards don't always need to be monetary; public acknowledgment, small tokens of appreciation, or even tying cyber performance to annual performance reviews or bonuses can be effective incentives. Gamifying security training is another approach that makes it more engaging and enjoyable for employees. Incorporating interactive scenarios, quizzes, or competitions encourages active participation in learning cyber best practices, increasing the likelihood that employees will retain and apply the information in their daily work

Question 6: What key metrics can we use to measure the effectiveness of our cyber program?

Answer: Measuring the effectiveness of your cyber program is essential for identifying areas for improvement and demonstrating the value of your cyber investments. One key metric to track is the number of reported phishing emails, as a high number indicates that employees are vigilant and aware of these types of attacks. Tracking this metric over time can help gauge the effectiveness of your security awareness training programs. Another important metric is the completion rate of mandatory security awareness training, ensuring that your workforce receives the necessary education to protect against cyber threats.

Monitoring patch management rates, or the percentage of up-to-date systems and applications with the latest security patches, can help identify potential vulnerabilities and ensure that your organization proactively addresses known security issues. Mean time to detect (MTTD) and mean time to respond (MTTR) are also crucial metrics, as they measure how quickly your organization detects and responds to security incidents. Reducing these times can help minimize the impact of a breach and demonstrate the effectiveness of your incident response plan.

While an entirely incident-free environment is unrealistic, tracking the number of security incidents over time can provide insight into the overall effectiveness of your cyber program as well as the types of attack that your organization is vulnerable to. A significant decrease in incidents may indicate an improvement in your cyber posture. Finally, tracking how your cyber budget is allocated across different initiatives, such as technology investments, employee training, and incident response, can help ensure that resources are used effectively and aligned with your organization's risk profile.

Question 7: How can we stay informed about the latest cyber threats and vulnerabilities?

Answer: Staying informed about the latest cyber threats and vulnerabilities is crucial for maintaining a strong cyber posture. Subscribing to reputable cyber publications and newsletters, such as SANS NewsBites, Threatpost, and Dark Reading, can provide regular updates on the latest threats, vulnerabilities, and best practices delivered directly to your inbox. Attending industry events and conferences like RSA Conference, Black Hat, and DEF CON offers valuable opportunities to learn about the latest trends, hear from industry experts, and network with other cyber professionals. Many of these events also provide virtual attendance options, making it easier to participate from anywhere.

Leveraging free online training resources from reputable sources like the SANS Institute, Cybrary, and the National Institute of Standards and Technology (NIST) Cyber Framework can help employees stay current on the latest cyber threats and best practices for defending against them. Participating in information-sharing initiatives, such as the Cyber Threat Alliance (CTA) or the Information Sharing and Analysis Centers (ISACs), provides access to timely and actionable threat intelligence, allowing organizations to share and receive information about emerging threats, vulnerabilities, and best practices for mitigating risks.

Engaging with online cyber communities, such as forums, social media groups, and subreddits, can provide valuable insights and discussions on the latest cyber threats and vulnerabilities from a mix of cyber professionals, researchers, and enthusiasts. Finally, fostering internal knowledge-sharing by encouraging your cyber team to share their knowledge and insights with the rest of the organization through regular updates, presentations, or newsletters helps ensure everyone understands the current threat landscape and the importance of cyber best practices.

Question 8: What role does cyber insurance play in our cyber strategy?

Answer: Cyber insurance can be a valuable tool for mitigating the financial impact of a cyber attack, helping to cover costs associated with data breach notification, legal fees, and business disruption. It allows organizations to transfer some of the financial risks associated with a cyber attack to an insurance provider, reducing the potential economic impact of a breach and providing access to resources and expertise to help manage the aftermath of an incident.

However, it's essential to understand that insurance does not replace a robust cyber program. Insurance companies will investigate claims and may deny coverage if they find that the organization was negligent in its cyber practices. For example, if an organization fails to implement basic security measures, such as regularly updating software or providing employee security training, an insurance provider may argue that the organization did not take reasonable steps to protect itself and deny coverage.

Therefore, the best approach is to focus on preventing cyber attacks in the first place through a comprehensive cyber program that includes risk assessments, employee training, and implementing strong technical controls. Cyber insurance should be viewed as a complement to, rather than a replacement for, these proactive measures.

When considering cyber insurance, it's crucial to carefully review the policy terms and conditions to understand what is covered and what is not. Some policies may have exclusions for certain types of attacks or may require the organization to meet specific cyber standards to qualify for coverage. Working closely with your insurance provider and legal counsel can help ensure your policy aligns with your organization's needs and risk profile.

Question 9: What are the ethical considerations surrounding cyber measures?

Answer: Cyber measures can sometimes raise ethical concerns regarding employee monitoring and data privacy. Organizations must balance protecting the company from cyber attacks and respecting employee privacy. Transparency is critical; employees have a right to know what types of monitoring are conducted and how their data is used. This can include monitoring email and internet usage and collecting and analyzing data from various sources to detect potential security threats.

Organizations should have clear policies to address these concerns regarding how employee data is collected, used, and protected. These policies should be communicated to employees and easily accessible. Employees should also be able to access their data and request corrections or deletions where appropriate. In addition, organizations should ensure that data is only collected and used for legitimate business purposes and that proper safeguards are in place to protect employee data from unauthorized access or misuse.

Another ethical consideration is using artificial intelligence (AI) and machine learning in cyber. While these technologies can be powerful tools for detecting and preventing cyber attacks, they can also raise concerns about bias and transparency. Organizations must ensure that AI systems are designed and trained to minimize bias and that their decision-making processes are transparent and explainable.

Finally, organizations must consider the ethical implications of their cyber measures on their customers and society. For example, collecting and storing large amounts of customer data can create risks if that data is breached or misused. Organizations are responsible for protecting customer data and using it ethically and responsibly.

In summary, ethical cyber practices involve balancing protecting the organization and respecting the privacy and rights of employees, customers, and society. By being transparent, implementing appropriate safeguards, and considering the ethical implications of their actions, organizations can create a strong cyber posture that is both effective and ethical.

Question 10: How can we ensure our cyber strategy remains relevant and effective in the face of constantly evolving threats?

Answer: The cyber landscape constantly evolves, with new threats and vulnerabilities emerging regularly. Adopting a proactive and adaptable approach is essential to ensure your cyber strategy remains relevant and practical. This starts with conducting regular risk assessments to identify new vulnerabilities and ensure that your existing cyber measures are still effective. These assessments should consider changes in your organization's technology infrastructure, business processes, and the broader threat landscape.

Based on the results of these assessments, your cyber strategy should be regularly updated and refined. This may involve implementing new security controls, updating policies and procedures, or investing in new technologies. It's essential to stay up-to-date with the latest trends and best practices in cyber and any changes in regulatory requirements or industry standards.

Investing in ongoing employee training and awareness programs is another critical aspect of maintaining an effective cyber strategy. As new threats emerge, employees must be equipped with the knowledge and skills to recognize and respond to them. Regular training sessions, simulated phishing exercises, and other awareness-building activities can help ensure that employees remain vigilant and prepared.

Collaboration and information sharing are also critical for staying ahead of evolving threats. Participating in industry groups, attending conferences and workshops, and engaging with cyber experts can provide valuable insights into emerging trends and best practices. Sharing information about threats and vulnerabilities with other organizations through formal information-sharing programs or informal networks can help create a more resilient and responsive cyber community.

Finally, it's essential to regularly test and validate your cyber strategy through exercises and simulations. This can include tabletop exercises, penetration testing, and other activities designed to assess the effectiveness of your controls and identify areas for improvement. By proactively identifying and addressing weaknesses in your strategy, you can ensure that your organization remains resilient and prepared in the face of evolving threats.

Further Reading

1. Singer, P. W., & Friedman, A. (2014). Cyber and cyberwar: What everyone needs to know. Oxford University Press.

2. Brenner, J. (2011). America the Vulnerable: Inside the new threat matrix of digital espionage, crime, and warfare. Penguin Press.

3. Schneier, B. (2015). Data and Goliath: The hidden battles to collect data and control your world. W. W. Norton & Company.

4. Kaplan, F. (2016). Dark territory: The secret history of cyber war. Simon & Schuster.

5. National Institute of Standards and Technology. (2018). Framework for improving critical infrastructure cyber, version 1.1. https://doi.org/10.6028/NIST.CSWP.04162018

Chapter 2

Applying Digital Risk Management For Business Optimization

Today, data is the most valuable asset for nearly all organizations. It fuels innovation, drives business growth, and fosters deeper customer relationships. However, this digital dependency also brings a heightened vulnerability to cyber risks. Just as a skilled navigator uses radar to detect hazards at sea, leaders require a thorough understanding of cyber risks to manage digital threats in today's business environment effectively.

This chapter sets the stage for digital risk management, which is essential for understanding the forthcoming discussions. It covers identifying and evaluating cyber threats, developing effective risk management strategies, and building trust with stakeholders through dedicated cyber efforts. By proactively managing cyber risk, you can optimize your business operations, protect your valuable assets, and seize the opportunities of the digital landscape. A cyber threat is a clearly defined activity or threat vector that by its existence creates a clear risk.

Unmasking Risks: The Executive's Cyber Radar

Consider your organization a busy cityscape. Its digital infrastructure flows with a constant data stream, including financial records, customer information, and intellectual property. However, potential threats lurk in the shadows, with cyber criminals seeking to exploit vulnerabilities and disrupt operations.

Identifying and assessing cyber risks is the first step toward effective management. This involves analyzing your digital assets, pinpointing potential vulnerabilities, and understanding the consequences of a successful attack. Several vital areas include people, processes, technology, and data.

Human error or social engineering attacks can be a significant entry point for cyber risks. Employees need to be aware of phishing tactics and data security best practices. Implementing multi-factor authentication adds an extra layer of protection beyond passwords. Inefficient or outdated security protocols can leave your IT systems vulnerable. Regularly reviewing your security policies and procedures ensures they address evolving risks. Conducting penetration testing simulates cyber attacks and identifies weaknesses in your defenses.

Outdated software, unpatched vulnerabilities, and unsecured devices can create opportunities for attackers. Implementing a rigorous patch management process and using security tools to monitor your network activity in real time is crucial. Segmenting your network can isolate critical systems and data. Sensitive information needs robust protection, so classifying your data based on sensitivity and implementing appropriate access controls and encryption measures is essential. Data loss prevention (DLP) solutions can prevent sensitive information from being inadvertently leaked.

By systematically examining these areas, you can build a comprehensive picture of your cyber risk landscape and prioritize threats based on their likelihood and potential impact.

The Evolving Threat Landscape: Why Constant Vigilance is Crucial

The digital threat landscape is dynamic, with cyber criminals constantly developing new methods and exploiting emerging technologies. Some key trends to be aware of include the rise of ransomware, supply chain attacks, the weaponization of AI and the Internet of Things (IoT).

Ransomware attacks encrypt a victim's data, rendering it inaccessible, and demand a ransom payment for decryption. These attacks can be particularly disruptive for businesses that rely heavily on their digital assets. For example, in July 2021, the REvil/Sodinokibi gang exploited a vulnerability in Kaseya VSA software to launch a significant ransomware attack affecting many of Kaseya's MSP clients and their downstream customers. The attackers initially demanded $70 million for a universal decryption key.

Hackers are increasingly targeting third-party vendors and partners to gain access to their target organizations' systems, which they can then use to launch attacks. In 2021, Accellion, a file-sharing and collaboration solutions provider, experienced breaches of its File Transfer Application. These breaches allowed attackers to access sensitive information from Accellion's clients, including primary healthcare and financial institutions. The incident showed how vulnerabilities in a third-party vendor's software could lead to widespread data exposure across different sectors that rely on this software for transferring and managing files securely.When evaluating potential vendors, it's essential to consider their cyber posture as part of the selection process.

Artificial intelligence can be used maliciously in various ways in cybersecurity. For example, AI-powered malware can learn and adapt to evade detection by traditional security systems. In 2018, researchers demonstrated an AI-driven malware called DeepLocker that could hide its malicious payload until it reached a specific target, making it extremely difficult to detect and prevent. Additionally, AI can automate social engineering attacks, such as phishing campaigns, by learning and mimicking human behavior to trick victims into revealing sensitive information. In 2021, researchers from Singapore discovered an AI-powered phishing campaign that used natural language processing to generate convincing fake emails tailored to specific individuals based on their publicly available information.

Furthermore, AI can be leveraged to launch more sophisticated and targeted denial-of-service attacks by learning and exploiting vulnerabilities in network infrastructure. While these examples are still relatively rare, they demonstrate the potential for AI to be used maliciously in the cyber domain. Staying informed about the latest developments in AI security and implementing safeguards to mitigate potential risks is crucial.

The proliferation of connected devices (IoT), from smart homes to industrial control systems, creates a vast attack surface for hackers to exploit. Securing these devices with strong passwords, keeping software updated, and turning off features that are not in use are essential. In February 2021, a cyber attack targeted a water treatment facility in Oldsmar, Florida, where an unauthorized entity attempted to access the water treatment facility's control system via an insecure sensor and increase the levels of sodium hydroxide in the water supply by a factor of 100. The attack was thwarted by an operator who noticed the anomaly, but it underscored the vulnerability of IoT devices in critical infrastructure.

The Cost of Inaction: Beyond Financial Losses

While the financial costs of a cyber attack can be significant, the damage goes beyond just lost revenue. A successful attack can have a devastating impact on your reputation and customer trust. Data breaches can lead to public scrutiny, regulatory fines, and lawsuits. Losing sensitive customer information can erode trust and loyalty, making it difficult to regain a foothold in the market. Furthermore, business disruptions caused by cyber attacks can damage your brand image and hinder your ability to compete effectively.

The hidden costs of a cyber attack can also extend to operational downtime, lost productivity, and incident response and recovery. For example, In 2022, Uber suffered a data breach that compromised the personal information of approximately 57 million users and 600,000 drivers. The hidden costs of this cyber attack extended beyond the immediate financial impact, as Uber faced operational downtime, lost productivity, and significant expenses related to incident response and recovery, including legal fees, credit monitoring services for affected individuals, and investments in enhanced cybersecurity measures. Whilst the full costs of this are not known, it is believed to exceed the $148 million actual costs of the 2016 breach at Uber.

Investing in robust cyber measures is not just an expense; it's a critical investment in protecting your organization's future. By proactively addressing cyber risks, you can minimize the potential for financial losses, reputational damage, and operational disruptions, ensuring your business's long-term health and success.

From Risk to Action

Recognizing the evolving risk landscape and the potential costs of a cyber attack is crucial, but it's only the first step in effective digital risk management. To mitigate these risks, organizations must move from awareness to action by implementing robust cybersecurity measures and fostering a culture of cyber resilience. This involves investing in technical solutions and engaging employees at all levels to create a shared sense of responsibility for protecting digital assets. By building strong lines of defense that start with behavior and culture, organizations can proactively address cyber threats and risks and minimize the impact of potential attacks. A comprehensive approach to digital risk management combines risk awareness, technical safeguards, and a culture of vigilance to create a resilient and secure digital environment.

Building a Culture of Cyber

Effective cyber goes beyond technical solutions. It requires a cultural shift within your organization, where everyone understands the importance of data security and plays a role in protecting your digital assets. Leadership commitment is crucial, with leaders setting the tone by demonstrating a strong commitment to cyber. This includes allocating resources, championing security initiatives, and holding employees accountable for data security practices. Leaders should also be visible advocates for cyber and communicate its importance to all levels of the organization.

Regular cyber training programs can equip employees with the knowledge and skills to identify risks, protect confidential information, and avoid social engineering attacks. Training should be engaging, relevant to employee roles, and updated regularly to address emerging risks. For example, Salesforce, a cloud-based customer relationship management (CRM) company, requires all employees to complete annual cyber training. The company also conducts regular phishing simulations to test employee awareness and identify areas for improvement.

Open communication about security concerns is essential, and employees should feel empowered to report suspicious activity without fear of reprisal. Fostering a culture of transparency is crucial for early detection and response to cyber risks. Creating channels for employees to report suspicious activity anonymously and investigating all reports promptly is essential.

A well-defined incident response plan is critical for minimizing the impact of a cyber attack. This plan should outline roles and responsibilities, communication protocols, and containment, eradication, and recovery steps. Regularly testing your plan ensures its effectiveness. For example, the National Institute of Standards and Technology (NIST) recommends conducting tabletop exercises to test incident response plans and identify areas for improvement.

Conclusion

Effective digital risk management requires a deep understanding of the threat landscape, including the rise of ransomware, supply chain attacks, and the weaponization of AI and IoT devices. However, awareness alone is not enough; organizations must take proactive steps to build strong lines of defense against these threats. This involves investing in robust technical solutions, such as multi-factor authentication, network segmentation, and data encryption, and fostering a culture of cyber resilience through employee training, open communication, and well-defined incident response plans. Organizations can effectively manage digital risks and protect their most valuable assets in an increasingly connected world by adopting a comprehensive approach that combines threat awareness, technical safeguards, and a culture of vigilance.

Answers To Key Questions

Question 1: What are the different types of cyber risks that organizations should be aware of?

Answer: Organizations face many cyber risks stemming from people, processes, technology, and data. Human error and social engineering attacks, such as phishing, pose significant risks. Employees need to be aware of phishing tactics and data security best practices. Inefficient or outdated security protocols can leave systems vulnerable, requiring regular reviews and updates. Outdated software, unpatched vulnerabilities, and unsecured devices create opportunities for attackers, making patch management and network monitoring crucial. Sensitive information needs robust protection through data classification, access controls, and encryption measures.

One type of cyber risk that organizations should be particularly aware of is insider threats. These risks come from within the organization, such as employees, contractors, or partners accessing sensitive data and systems. Insider threats can be malicious, such as an employee stealing data or sabotaging systems, or unintentional, such as an employee falling victim to a phishing scam and inadvertently giving attackers access to the network.

Another type of cyber risk is third-party risk. Many organizations rely on external vendors, suppliers, and partners to support their operations. However, these third parties can introduce additional risks if their cyber practices are not up to par. A breach at a third-party vendor could expose your organization's data or provide an entry point for attackers to infiltrate your systems.

To mitigate these risks, organizations must adopt a comprehensive approach to cyber that addresses the human element, strengthens processes secures technology, and safeguards data. This includes providing regular employee training, implementing strong access controls and data protection measures, and conducting thorough risk assessments of third-party partners.

Question 2: How can organizations identify and assess their cyber risks?

Answer: Identifying and assessing cyber risks is the foundation of an effective risk management strategy. The first step is to thoroughly inventory your digital assets, including hardware, software, and data. This involves cataloging all devices, applications, and databases that store or process sensitive information and identifying who has access to these assets and how they are currently protected.

Once you have a clear picture of your digital ecosystem, the next step is to perform vulnerability assessments and penetration testing. Vulnerability assessments involve scanning your systems and applications for known security weaknesses, such as unpatched software vulnerabilities or misconfigurations. Penetration testing, however, involves actively exploiting these vulnerabilities to identify potential entry points for attackers.

Your security team can conduct these assessments internally or by engaging third-party experts specializing in identifying and assessing cyber risks. The results of these assessments will provide a prioritized list of vulnerabilities that need to be addressed, along with recommendations for remediation.

Another critical aspect of risk assessment is evaluating each identified risk's likelihood and potential impact. This involves considering factors such as the sensitivity of the data involved, the possible financial and reputational consequences of a breach, and the effectiveness of existing security controls. By quantifying these risks, organizations can prioritize their remediation efforts and allocate resources accordingly.

It's important to note that risk assessment is not a one-time exercise. As the risk landscape evolves and new vulnerabilities emerge, organizations must regularly reassess their risks to ensure their cyber posture remains effective. This continuous process of identifying, assessing, and mitigating risks is essential for staying ahead of potential risks and minimizing the impact of any incidents that do occur.

Question 3: What are some key considerations when developing a cyber risk management strategy?

Answer: Developing a comprehensive cyber risk management strategy requires a multifaceted approach considering various factors and stakeholders within the organization. One key consideration is aligning the cyber strategy with overall business objectives. Cyber should not be viewed as a standalone function but as an enabler of business success. By understanding how cyber risks can impact strategic goals, such as revenue growth, customer acquisition, or market expansion, organizations can prioritize their cyber investments and ensure that they support rather than hinder business objectives.

Another essential factor to consider is the organization's risk appetite and tolerance. Some organizations, such as those in highly regulated industries like healthcare or finance, may have a very low tolerance for cyber risk and require stringent security controls. Others may be willing to accept a higher level of risk in exchange for greater flexibility or innovation. Defining the organization's risk appetite upfront helps guide decision-making and ensures the cyber risk management strategy is aligned with the overall risk profile.

Effective cyber risk management also requires buy-in and participation from stakeholders, not just the IT or security teams. This includes engaging with business unit leaders, legal and compliance teams, human resources, and even the board of directors. Each stakeholder brings a unique perspective and requirements to consider when developing the strategy. For example, the legal team may have specific requirements around data privacy and regulatory compliance, while human resources may be focused on employee training and awareness.

Once the strategy is developed, it's essential to establish clear metrics and key performance indicators (KPIs) to measure its effectiveness over time. This can include tracking the number of security incidents, the time it takes to detect and respond to threats, and the overall reduction in cyber risk exposure. Regular reporting on these metrics helps keep stakeholders informed and ensures the strategy remains practical and relevant as the risk landscape evolves.

Finally, it's important to remember that cyber risk management is not a one-size-fits-all approach. Each organization has unique risks, assets, and priorities to consider when developing a strategy. Companies can effectively manage their cyber risks and build a more resilient and secure digital ecosystem by taking a tailored, risk-based approach that aligns with business objectives and engages stakeholders across the organization.

Question 4: What are the potential consequences of a cyber attack beyond financial losses?

Answer: While the financial costs of a cyber attack can be significant, the consequences often extend far beyond monetary losses. One of the most severe impacts is reputational damage. In today's digital age, trust is critical for any organization. Customers, partners, and investors expect companies to safeguard their sensitive data and maintain the integrity of their systems. A high-profile data breach or security incident can severely erode that trust, leading to lost business, decreased customer loyalty, and even legal action.

For example, the 2017 Equifax data breach, which exposed the personal information of over 147 million people, devastated the company's reputation. In addition to the immediate financial costs of the breach, including legal fees, regulatory fines, and customer notification expenses, Equifax faced significant backlash from consumers and policymakers. The company's stock price plummeted, and it faced intense scrutiny from regulators and lawmakers, leading to the resignation of several top executives.

Beyond reputational damage, cyber attacks can also have serious operational consequences. In the case of a ransomware attack, for example, an organization's critical systems and data may be encrypted and held hostage until a ransom is paid. This can result in significant downtime, lost productivity, and missed business opportunities. Even after the ransom is paid and systems are restored, there may be lingering effects, such as data corruption or the need to rebuild systems from scratch.

Cyber attacks can also have legal and regulatory implications, particularly if sensitive data is compromised. Depending on the industry and jurisdiction, organizations may be subject to mandatory breach notification laws, which require them to inform customers and regulators of any security incidents that involve personal data. Failure to comply with these laws can result in significant fines and legal action.

Finally, cyber attacks can profoundly impact an organization's workforce. If their data is compromised, employees may feel a sense of violation or betrayal, leading to decreased morale and productivity. Employees may even face personal consequences, such as identity theft or financial fraud, due to a breach.

To mitigate these risks, organizations must prioritize cyber as a critical business function and invest in the people, processes, and technologies needed to prevent, detect, and respond to cyber risks. By taking a proactive and holistic approach to cyber, organizations can minimize the potential consequences of an attack and build a more resilient and secure digital ecosystem.

Question 5: How can organizations build a culture of cyber?

Answer: Building a strong cyber culture is essential for any organization looking to protect its digital assets and maintain the trust of its stakeholders. A cyber culture goes beyond simply implementing technical controls or providing employee training. It requires a fundamental shift in mindset, where every individual within the organization understands their role in protecting sensitive data and maintaining the integrity of systems.

Leadership commitment is one of the most critical factors in building a cyber culture. Senior executives and board members must prioritize cyber as a critical business issue and allocate the necessary resources and attention to address it. This includes setting the tone from the top by regularly communicating the importance of cyber, modeling good security behaviors, and holding individuals accountable for their actions.

Another critical element of a strong cyber culture is employee engagement and education. All employees, regardless of their role or technical expertise, should receive regular training on cyber best practices, such as identifying and reporting phishing emails, creating strong passwords, and handling sensitive data appropriately. This training should be engaging, interactive, and tailored to the organization's needs and risks.

In addition to formal training, organizations should foster open communication and collaboration around cyber. Employees should feel comfortable reporting potential security incidents or vulnerabilities without fear of retribution. They should also be encouraged to share their own experiences and insights, as this can help identify areas for improvement and build a sense of shared responsibility for cyber.

Organizations can also leverage technology to reinforce good cyber behaviors and make it easier for employees to do the right thing. For example, implementing multi-factor authentication or password management tools can help ensure employees use strong, unique passwords across all their accounts. Similarly, data loss prevention (DLP) tools can help prevent sensitive data from being accidentally or intentionally leaked outside the organization. Data Loss Prevention (DLP) tools are software solutions designed to detect, monitor, and prevent the unauthorized transmission of sensitive or critical data outside an organization's network. These tools help organizations safeguard their valuable information assets by enforcing data security policies and preventing breaches.

For example, an employee attempts to send an email containing confidential customer information to an external recipient. The organization's DLP tool scans the email content, configured to monitor and block the unauthorized sharing of sensitive data. Upon detecting the confidential information, the DLP tool automatically prevents the email from being sent and alerts the IT security team. The employee is notified that the email violates the company's data security policy. This real-time intervention helps prevent sensitive data's accidental or malicious leakage, protecting the organization from potential data breaches and compliance issues.

Finally, organizations should regularly assess and measure the effectiveness of their cyber culture through metrics such as employee training completion rates, phishing simulation click rates, and the number of reported security incidents. This data can help identify areas for improvement and track progress over time. A cultural audit can help to provide vulnerabilities within the organization.

By taking a holistic and proactive approach to building a cyber culture, organizations can create a more resilient and secure digital ecosystem that engages employees, protects sensitive data, and maintains the trust of stakeholders.

Question 6: What are some best practices for implementing multi-factor authentication (MFA)?

Answer: Implementing multi-factor authentication (MFA) is a crucial step in enhancing the security of an organization's digital assets. MFA adds an extra layer of protection beyond traditional usernames and passwords by requiring users to provide additional verification factors, such as a fingerprint, a one-time code sent to their mobile device, or a hardware token.

One of the first considerations when implementing MFA is determining which systems and applications require this additional level of security. While it may be tempting to apply MFA universally, this can create friction for users and may not be necessary for all resources. Instead, organizations should prioritize MFA for critical systems that contain sensitive data or provide access to high-value assets.

Another best practice is to provide users with multiple options for the second authentication factor. While SMS-based one-time codes are popular, they can be vulnerable to interception or social engineering attacks. Alternatives like hardware tokens or authenticator apps can provide users with more secure and convenient options.

It's also important to consider the user experience when implementing MFA. If the process is too cumbersome or time-consuming, users may try to circumvent it or become frustrated, decreasing productivity. Organizations should strive to make the MFA process seamless and intuitive, providing clear instructions and support for users unfamiliar with the technology.

Another critical consideration is the management and security of the MFA system itself. Organizations should choose a reputable and well-established MFA provider that follows industry best practices for security and data privacy. They should also have processes for securely provisioning and revoking MFA credentials and monitoring and responding to suspicious activity.

Finally, organizations should provide adequate training and communication around implementing MFA. Users should understand why MFA is being implemented, how it works, and what to do if they encounter any issues. This can help build buy-in and ensure users are comfortable and confident using the new system.

By following these best practices, organizations can effectively implement MFA as part of a comprehensive cyber strategy, providing an additional layer of protection for their most critical assets and data.

Question 7: What are the benefits of conducting penetration testing for cyber?

Answer: Penetration testing, or ethical hacking, is a critical component of a comprehensive cyber strategy. It involves simulating real-world cyber attacks against an organization's systems and networks to identify vulnerabilities and weaknesses that malicious actors could exploit.

One of the primary benefits of conducting penetration testing is that it provides a deep and realistic assessment of an organization's security posture. Unlike automated vulnerability scans or theoretical risk assessments, penetration testing involves actively attempting to breach an organization's defenses using the same tactics and techniques that real-world attackers employ. This can uncover hidden vulnerabilities or misconfigurations that might go unnoticed, such as weak passwords, unpatched software, or insecure network configurations.

Another critical benefit of penetration testing is that it helps organizations prioritize their security investments and remediation efforts. By identifying the most critical vulnerabilities and demonstrating the potential impact of a successful attack, penetration testing can help security teams focus their resources on the areas that pose the most significant risk to the organization. This can help ensure that limited security budgets are allocated effectively and efficiently.

Penetration testing can also help organizations assess the effectiveness of their existing security controls and incident response capabilities. By simulating a real-world attack, penetration testing can test an organization's ability to detect, respond to, and recover from a security incident. This can identify gaps or weaknesses in an organization's incident response plan, allowing them to be addressed before an actual attack occurs.

In addition to these technical benefits, penetration testing can provide valuable insights into an organization's security culture and awareness. By attempting to breach an organization's defenses through social engineering tactics, such as phishing emails or phone calls, penetration testers can assess the effectiveness of employee security training and identify areas where additional education or awareness may be needed.

Finally, penetration testing can help organizations demonstrate their commitment to cyber to customers, partners, and regulators. Many industries have specific compliance requirements around security testing, such as the Payment Card Industry Data Security Standard (PCI DSS) for organizations that process credit card transactions. By conducting regular penetration testing and addressing any identified vulnerabilities, organizations can show that they are taking proactive steps to protect sensitive data and maintain the trust of their stakeholders.

Overall, penetration testing is invaluable for any organization looking to strengthen its cyber posture and build a more resilient and secure digital ecosystem. By providing a realistic assessment of an organization's vulnerabilities, prioritizing remediation efforts, and testing incident response capabilities, penetration testing can help organizations stay ahead of evolving cyber threats and maintain the trust of their customers and stakeholders.

Question 8: How can organizations leverage data loss prevention (DLP) solutions to mitigate cyber risks?

Answer: Data loss prevention (DLP) solutions are critical for organizations looking to protect sensitive data from unauthorized access, use, or disclosure. DLP solutions monitor and control data in motion, at rest, and in use across an organization's networks, endpoints, and applications. They can help prevent data breaches, ensure compliance with regulatory requirements, and protect intellectual property.

One key benefit of DLP solutions is that they provide visibility into how sensitive data is being used and accessed across the organization. By monitoring data in motion, at rest, and in use, DLP solutions can help organizations identify potential security risks, such as employees sending sensitive data to personal email accounts or storing confidential information on unsecured devices. This visibility can help organizations take proactive steps to mitigate these risks, such as implementing additional security controls or providing targeted employee training.

Another critical aspect of DLP solutions is their ability to enforce security policies and prevent unauthorized data transfers. DLP solutions can be configured to block or quarantine data that violates predefined rules, such as attempting to send sensitive data outside the organization or accessing confidential information from an unsecured network. This can help organizations prevent data breaches and ensure that sensitive data remains secure.

DLP solutions can also help organizations classify and prioritize their data based on its level of sensitivity and criticality. By identifying and tagging data according to its level of confidentiality, organizations can apply appropriate security controls and monitoring based on the risk associated with each data type. This can help organizations focus their security efforts on the most critical data assets and ensure that resources are allocated effectively.

When implementing DLP solutions, organizations should take a risk-based approach that balances security with business needs. While it may be tempting to lock down all data and prevent unauthorized transfers, this can create significant barriers to productivity and collaboration. Instead, organizations should work with business stakeholders to identify the most critical data assets and develop policies and procedures that balance security with operational efficiency.

Organizations should also consider integrating DLP solutions with other security tools and platforms, such as security information and event management (SIEM) systems and incident response workflows. Organizations can more quickly detect and respond to potential security incidents involving sensitive data by correlating data from multiple sources and automating response actions.

In 2020, the University of Utah Health (U of U Health) reported that their DLP tool successfully prevented a data breach. The DLP software detected an unusual download of sensitive information, including patient data, by a former employee. The tool alerted the IT security team, who promptly investigated the incident and found that the former employee had downloaded the data without authorization.

U of U Health's quick response, enabled by the DLP tool's real-time detection capabilities, allowed them to secure the downloaded data and prevent any further unauthorized access or disclosure. The organization reported that no patient information was compromised due to the incident.

According to the official statement released by U of U Health, "The DLP software worked as intended and detected the downloading of the sensitive information, which assisted the University's IT Security team and the University of Utah Police Department in identifying the downloaded data and the employee."

Finally, organizations should provide adequate training and communication around implementing DLP solutions. Employees should understand why DLP is being implemented, how it works, and their responsibilities for protecting sensitive data. This can help build buy-in and ensure that employees know the importance of data security.

By leveraging DLP solutions as part of a comprehensive data security strategy, organizations can gain greater visibility into the use and movement of sensitive data, enforce security policies, and reduce the risk of data breaches. This can help organizations protect their most valuable assets, ensure compliance with regulatory requirements, and maintain the trust of their customers and stakeholders.

Question 9: How can cyber be integrated into digital transformation initiatives?

Answer: Digital transformation initiatives, such as the adoption of cloud computing, mobile technologies, and the Internet of Things (IoT), are rapidly changing the way organizations operate and deliver value to their customers. However, these initiatives also introduce new security risks and challenges that must be addressed to protect sensitive data and systems.

To effectively integrate cyber into digital transformation initiatives, organizations should take a proactive and holistic approach that considers security at every stage. This starts with conducting thorough security assessments of new technologies and platforms before deployment. These assessments should identify potential vulnerabilities and risks and provide recommendations for mitigating them by implementing appropriate security controls.

Organizations should also prioritize security as a fundamental design principle in developing new applications and services. This means incorporating security requirements and testing into the software development lifecycle and ensuring that security is considered at every stage, from initial design to deployment and ongoing maintenance. By building security into the fabric of new digital initiatives, organizations can reduce the risk of vulnerabilities and ensure that security is an integral part of the overall user experience.

Question 10: How should we communicate cyber risks to different audiences, such as The Board, Employees, and Customers?

Answer: Effectively communicating cyber risks to different audiences - such as the board, employees, and customers - requires tailored approaches to ensure understanding and buy-in.

For the Board: Emphasize the financial and reputational impacts of cyber risks. Use clear business language that aligns cyber with business objectives. Present data-driven insights, such as risk assessments and trend analyses, to support investment in cyber measures. It's critical to frame discussions around risk management and strategic decision-making, focusing on the potential consequences of inaction.

For Employees: Simplify the technical aspects of cyber risks and focus on practical implications. Use relatable scenarios to demonstrate how specific behaviors can lead to breaches. Interactive training sessions, such as workshops and simulations, can be particularly effective. It's essential to foster a security culture by making employees feel like an integral part of the company's defenses, encouraging vigilance and responsibility.

For Customers: Maintain transparency while ensuring communications are reassuring, avoiding unnecessary technical jargon. Explain what measures are in place to protect their data and how they can contribute to security (e.g., password practices, recognizing phishing attempts). Regular updates about security improvements and quick, clear communication about any breaches are crucial for maintaining trust.

Visual aids such as charts, graphs, and infographics can effectively illustrate risks and defenses across all groups. Regular updates, whether through newsletters, briefs, or meetings, help keep cyber front and center. Ultimately, the key is to make the information accessible and relevant, ensuring that each audience understands their role in the broader context of cyber risk management. Building this understanding helps achieve awareness and active participation in mitigating cyber risks.

Further Reading

1. Hubbard, D. W., & Seiersen, R. (2016). How to measure anything in cyber risk. Wiley.

2. Kosutic, D. (2017). Secure & straightforward: A small-business guide to implementing ISO 27001 independently. IT Governance Publishing.

3. National Institute of Standards and Technology. (2020). NIST special publication 800-37, revision 2: Risk management

framework for information systems and organizations: A system life cycle approach for security and privacy. https://doi.org/10.6028/NIST.SP.800-37r2

4. Radichel, T. (2014). Case study: Critical controls that could have prevented Target breach. SANS Institute. https://www.sans.org/reading-room/whitepapers/casestudies/case-study-critical-controls-prevented-target-breach-35412

5. Sommer, P., & Brown, I. (2011). Reducing systemic cyber risk. Organization for Economic Cooperation and Development (OECD). https://doi.org/10.1787/5kgdvnq8zx8v-en

Chapter 3

Creating A Cyber Strategy Roadmap For Business

A robust cyber strategy is imperative for businesses in today's digital age. Creating a strategy that effectively protects your organization's valuable assets must be firmly grounded in your business objectives. Start by defining your organization's strategic goals for the next few years. Are you aiming to expand into new markets, launch innovative products, or improve operational efficiency? Once you have identified these goals, thoroughly analyze how cyber threats could disrupt or derail them.

For example, if your objective is to expand into new markets, a successful cyber attack that exposes sensitive customer data could lead to regulatory fines, loss of trust, and significant reputational damage, hindering your expansion efforts. By understanding the potential impact of cyber risks on your business goals, you can prioritize your cyber investments accordingly. Focus on the areas that address the most critical risks and contribute significantly to safeguarding your ability to achieve your objectives. This alignment ensures that your cyber strategy is not just a technical exercise but a business-driven initiative that actively protects your organization's success.

Communicating Strategy Across Your Organization

Effective communication is crucial for the successful implementation of your cyber strategy. Leaders play a vital role in championing the strategy, as their commitment and clear communication set the tone for the entire organization. They can demonstrate this commitment by actively participating in training sessions, leading by example, and regularly communicating the importance of cyber through various channels.

To ensure your message reaches all employees, regardless of location or technical background, utilize various communication methods. This may include town hall meetings, training sessions (both in-person and online), email newsletters, internal knowledge-sharing platforms, and even digital signage within the workplace. Tailor your messages to different audience segments, providing technical teams with in-depth details while offering general employees simplified explanations focusing on the importance of cyber and their roles.

Remember, cyber awareness is an ongoing process. Regularly communicate updates, reminders about best practices, and real-world examples of cyber threats to keep cyber top-of-mind for all employees. Conduct phishing simulations and awareness campaigns to test employee preparedness and identify areas for improvement. By implementing a comprehensive communication strategy, you can foster a culture of cyber where everyone understands their role in maintaining a secure digital environment.

Avoiding Cyber Complexity

While cyber can seem complex and ever-evolving, there are steps you can take to keep your strategy clear and accessible for all employees. Focus on core cyber principles that everyone should understand, such as strong passwords, password managers, multi-factor authentication (MFA), data classification, and reporting suspicious activity. These principles are essential for all employees, regardless of their technical expertise.

Utilize visual aids like infographics, flowcharts, and videos to explain complex security concepts in an engaging and easy-to-understand manner. These visuals can be beneficial in depicting security processes, attack scenarios, and the consequences of cyber breaches. Tailor training to different employee groups' specific roles and responsibilities, ensuring they receive information most relevant to their daily tasks and how they can contribute to cyber efforts.

Consider gamifying cyber training to make it more interactive and engaging, especially for non-technical users. Gamification can involve incorporating points, badges, and leaderboards into training modules, adding an element of competition and recognition to motivate employees to participate and actively retain information. However, ensure that the gamified elements complement the learning objectives and maintain the seriousness of cyber practices.

Conducting Regular Cyber Strategy Reviews

Regularly reviewing your cyber strategy to ensure its continued effectiveness is essential in today's dynamic business environment. Establish a schedule for these reviews, which could be annually, semi-annually, or even quarterly, depending on the pace of change in your business and the current state of cyber threats.

During these reviews, re-evaluate your organization's strategic goals and assess emerging cyber threats. Consider whether your business model has changed and whether new industry regulations or compliance requirements impact your security posture. Evaluate the effectiveness of your current cyber strategy in mitigating identified risks and achieving your business objectives, looking for any gaps or areas that need adjustment.

Based on your review findings, adapt and improve your cyber

strategy as needed. This could involve updating security policies, allocating additional resources, or implementing new technologies. Regular reviews ensure that your cyber strategy remains aligned with your evolving business needs and the dynamic nature of cyber threats.

Balancing Cyber Investments with Business Needs

While cyber investments are crucial, they must be balanced with other strategic business needs. Conduct a cost-benefit analysis for potential cyber investments, evaluating the likely financial impact of a cyber attack against the cost of implementing a specific security measure. This helps prioritize investments based on the potential "Return on Security Investment" (RoSI).

It's also important to consider the "Risk of Not Investing" (RoNI). Before ruling out an investment, consider the second and third-order effects of not investing and the possible impacts on your supporting ecosystem. Adopt a risk-based approach that focuses cyber investments on mitigating your organization's most critical risks. Not all threats require the same level of investment, so prioritize controls that address high-impact and high-likelihood threats.

Explore ways to leverage existing resources before investing in entirely new solutions. Can existing security tools be used more effectively? Can internal expertise be leveraged to address specific security needs? By taking a cost-conscious and risk-based approach, you can ensure that your cyber investments align with your overall business strategy and deliver maximum value. Remember, cyber should enable your business, not hinder it.

Updating Strategy in Response to New Threats

Cyber threats are constantly evolving, and new threats emerge regularly. Your cyber strategy must be adaptable to address these threats effectively. In the previous chapter, we talked about the risk mitigation actions that can be taken, including implementing a threat intelligence program to stay informed about the latest cyber threats and vulnerabilities. Because the risks will constantly be evolving, you need to have a process by which these can then be validated against the strategy, and where appropriate to adapt the strategy to overcome the new risks. This will allow you to proactively update your defenses and address new risks before they can be exploited.

A key component of the strategy must therefore be how you keep the iteration going between assessing, monitoring and tackling emerging risks, and keeping the strategy relevant. This does not mean that the strategy changes daily or weekly - far from it. The strategy should stand the test of time, but it is important to have regular feedback loops to ensure that the strategy maintains and ideally, increases your capability to deal with incidents. For example, your strategy should include how you maintain a well-defined incident response plan that outlines procedures for detecting, responding to, and recovering from a cyber attack. Regularly testing and updating this plan to reflect the current state of cyber threats should be clearly called out in your strategy.

Measuring the Success of Your Strategy

Measuring the success of your cyber strategy goes beyond simply avoiding cyber attacks. Track the number of security incidents detected and the effectiveness of your response. A decrease in incidents may indicate an improvement in your security posture. Monitor the rate at which identified vulnerabilities are patched or addressed. A high remediation rate suggests you're proactively managing security weaknesses.

Track employee participation in cyber training and assess their understanding of security best practices. Regular awareness campaigns can help improve these metrics. While difficult to quantify precisely, consider the potential cost savings associated with preventing a cyber attack. This can help demonstrate your cyber efforts' "Return on Investment" (ROI). By tracking these metrics, you can gain valuable insights into your cyber strategy's effectiveness and identify areas for improvement.

The Role of Leadership in Driving the Cyber Agenda

Leadership plays a critical role in driving the cyber agenda within an organization. Leaders set the tone for the organization's cyber culture, and their commitment to adhering to security practices sends a powerful message to employees. They can demonstrate this commitment by actively participating in cyber awareness campaigns, championing security initiatives, and allocating the necessary resources to implement and maintain an effective cyber strategy.

Leaders should also set clear and strategic Key Performance Indicators (KPI) instead of just holding employees accountable for adhering to cyber policies and procedures. The KPI can be monitored and discussed, with clear actions recorded to ensure they are met. Where necessary, if individual performance is blocking the achievement of those KPIs, then re-establishing attainment can be achieved through performance reviews, disciplinary actions, and positive reinforcement for secure practices. Leaders should lead by example regarding cyber, using strong passwords, practising good email hygiene, and being cautious about clicking suspicious links. By demonstrating these behaviors, leaders set a positive standard for the rest of the organization. For example at BP plc, individuals had a cyber scorecard that reflected their adherence to security policies, reporting of suspicious emails, avoidance of opening infected emails and other cyber metrics. These dashboards rolled up by team and then by business unit so there was full transparency over which teams and individuals scored highly each month. These scores then formed part of the group bonus metrics.

Engaging with External Partners

Engaging with external partners can significantly enhance your organization's overall security posture. Managed Security Service Providers (MSSPs) offer various security services, including monitoring, threat detection, and incident response. They can provide valuable expertise and resources to supplement your internal security team.

Collaborating with cyber vendors can help you stay informed about the latest threats and solutions. Vendors can provide valuable insights and recommendations to strengthen your defenses. Participating in industry associations allows you to share best practices and learn from other organizations' experiences. These associations can also be a valuable source of threat intelligence.

Maintain open communication channels with law enforcement agencies. Collaborating with law enforcement can be crucial for investigating and recovering from a cyber attack. You can leverage their expertise and resources to bolster your organization's cyber defenses by engaging with external partners.

Conclusion

Creating a successful cyber strategy roadmap requires a holistic approach that aligns with your business objectives, is effectively communicated across the organization, and fosters a culture of cyber. Regular reviews, adaptation to evolving threats, and continuous improvement are essential for maintaining a strong cyber posture in today's dynamic digital landscape. Following the principles outlined in this chapter, you can create a robust cyber strategy that protects your valuable assets and enables your organization to achieve its strategic goals.

Answers To Key Questions

Question 1: How is our cyber strategy aligned with our business objectives?

Answer: Conduct a gap analysis to align your cyber strategy with your business objectives effectively. Review your organization's strategic objectives for the next few years, whether they focus on market expansion, product innovation, or operational efficiency improvements. Identify potential cyber threats that could disrupt or derail these goals. For instance, a data breach during a market expansion phase could erode customer trust and hinder your efforts.

Assess how your cyber strategy addresses these identified risks, looking for gaps or areas where your security measures don't adequately protect your ability to achieve your business objectives. Prioritize your cyber investments based on their potential impact on your business goals, focusing on areas that address the most critical risks and contribute significantly to safeguarding your ability to achieve your objectives.

Conducting this gap analysis can identify misalignments between your cyber strategy and business goals, allowing you to make necessary adjustments to ensure your security efforts actively protect your organization's success. Remember, effective cyber measures should always be business-enabling, not hindering.

Question 2: What channels and methods are we using to communicate our cyber strategy effectively across the organization?

Answer: Effective communication of your cyber strategy requires a multi-channel approach to reach all employees. Utilize diverse communication channels to cater to employee preferences and locations, such as town hall meetings, training sessions (both in-person and online), email newsletters, internal knowledge-sharing platforms, and even digital signage within the workplace.

Craft clear and concise messages tailored to different audience segments. Technical teams might require in-depth details about specific technologies or vulnerabilities, while general employees might benefit from simplified explanations focusing on the importance of cyber and their roles. Leadership engagement is crucial, with leaders playing a pivotal role in championing cyber strategies through regular communication channels, active participation in training sessions, and clear communication that sets the tone for the organization and motivates employees to embrace secure practices.

Cyber awareness is not a one-time event, so regularly communicate updates, reminders about best practices, and real-world cyber threat examples to keep cyber top-of-mind for all employees. Conduct phishing simulations and awareness campaigns to test employee preparedness and identify areas for improvement. By implementing a comprehensive communication strategy that leverages various channels, tailors content, and emphasizes leadership engagement, you can ensure everyone in your organization understands their role in maintaining a secure digital environment.

Question 3: How do we ensure our cyber strategy remains understandable to all employees, regardless of their technical expertise?

Answer: Imagine a workplace where every employee, from the IT specialist to the marketing professional, is well-versed in cyber best practices. To achieve this goal, your cyber strategy must be clear, accessible, and engaging to all, regardless of technical background.

Begin by focusing on the core cyber principles everyone needs to understand, such as using strong passwords, password managers, multi-factor authentication (MFA), data classification practices, and reporting suspicious activity. These foundational elements form the bedrock of a secure organization.

To effectively convey your strategy, leverage visuals like infographics, flowcharts, and videos to explain complex security concepts in a digestible and engaging manner. These visuals can be particularly useful when illustrating security processes, attack scenarios, and the potential consequences of cyber breaches, making the information more memorable and impactful.

It is also crucial to tailor your training to different employee groups based on their specific roles and responsibilities. By providing information that is directly relevant to their daily tasks, you can ensure that employees understand how their actions contribute to the organization's overall cyber efforts.

Furthermore, consider incorporating gamification elements into your training modules to increase employee engagement and motivation. By adding points, badges, and leaderboards, you can create a sense of competition and recognition that encourages active participation and information retention. However, it is essential to ensure that these gamified elements complement the learning objectives and maintain the gravity of cyber practices.

By focusing on core principles, utilizing engaging visuals, tailoring training, and potentially incorporating gamification, you can develop a cyber strategy that is not only understandable but also engaging for all employees. This approach will foster a culture of cyber awareness and responsibility throughout your organization, ultimately strengthening your overall security posture.

Question 4: Are we conducting regular cyber strategy reviews to align with changing business goals?

Answer: Regular reviews are crucial to ensure your cyber strategy remains effective despite evolving business goals and the ever-changing threat landscape. Establish a regular schedule for reviewing your cyber strategy, which could be annually, semi-annually, or even quarterly, depending on the pace of change in your business and the current state of cyber threats.

During these reviews, re-evaluate your organization's strategic goals and assess emerging cyber threats. Consider whether your business model has changed and whether new industry regulations or compliance requirements impact your security posture. Evaluate how well your current strategy mitigates identified risks and helps achieve your business objectives, looking for gaps or areas where your strategy needs to be adjusted.

Based on your review findings, adapt and improve your cyber strategy as needed. This could involve updating security policies, allocating additional resources, or implementing new technologies. Regular reviews ensure that your cyber strategy remains aligned with your changing business goals and the dynamic nature of cyber threats.

Question 5: How do we balance cyber investments with other strategic business needs?

Answer: Balancing cyber investments with other business priorities requires a strategic approach. Conduct a cost-benefit analysis to evaluate potential cyber investments, considering the likely financial impact of a cyber attack against the cost of implementing a specific security measure. This helps prioritize investments based on the potential "Return on Security Investment" (RoSI).

It's also important to consider the "Risk of Not Investing" (RoNI). Before ruling out an investment, consider the second and third-order effects of not investing and the possible impacts on your supporting ecosystem. Adopt a risk-based approach that focuses cyber investments on mitigating your organization's most critical risks. Not all threats require the same level of investment, so prioritize controls that address high-impact and high-likelihood threats.

Explore ways to leverage existing resources before investing in entirely new solutions, such as using existing security tools more effectively or leveraging internal expertise to address specific security needs. By optimizing existing resources, you can address security gaps without significant additional expenditure. A cost-conscious, risk-based approach ensures that your cyber investments align with your overall business strategy and deliver maximum value, demonstrating a commitment to security while keeping costs manageable.

Question 6: What is the process for updating our cyber strategy in response to new threats?

Answer: To ensure your cyber strategy remains effective in the face of an evolving threat landscape, implement a process for updating your plan in response to new threats. Start by implementing a threat intelligence program to stay informed about the latest cyber threats and vulnerabilities. This allows you to proactively update your defenses and address new risks before they can be exploited.

Threat intelligence can come from various sources, including industry reports, security vendors, and law enforcement agencies. Develop and maintain a well-defined incident response plan that outlines procedures for detecting, responding to, and recovering from a cyber attack. This plan should be regularly tested and updated to reflect the current cyber threats, helping you minimize damage and downtime during an attack.

Regularly assess and promptly patch your systems and applications for vulnerabilities, as unpatched vulnerabilities are a significant entry point for attackers. By prioritizing vulnerability management, you can significantly reduce your attack surface. By staying informed about emerging threats and implementing proactive measures, you can ensure your cyber strategy remains effective in a constantly evolving threat landscape.

Question 7: How are we measuring the success of our cyber strategy?

Answer: Measuring the success of your cyber strategy involves tracking key metrics beyond simply avoiding cyber attacks. Track the number of security incidents detected and the effectiveness of your response. A decrease in incidents may indicate an improvement in your security posture, but it's important to note that a lack of detected incidents doesn't necessarily mean no attacks were attempted.

Monitor the rate at which identified vulnerabilities are patched or addressed. A high remediation rate suggests you're proactively managing security weaknesses. Track employee participation in cyber training and assess their understanding of security best practices. Regular awareness campaigns can help improve these metrics.

While difficult to quantify precisely, consider the potential cost savings associated with preventing a cyber attack. This can help demonstrate your cyber efforts' return on investment (ROI). Remember, the cost of a successful attack can be significant, including financial losses, reputational damage, and regulatory fines.

By regularly monitoring these metrics, you can gain valuable insights into your cyber strategy's effectiveness and identify areas for improvement. Regular measurement also allows you to demonstrate the value of your security program to stakeholders and make data-driven decisions about future investments and priorities.

Question 8: What is the role of leadership in driving the cyber agenda?

Answer: Leadership plays a critical role in fostering a strong cyber culture within an organization. Leaders set the tone for the organization's cyber culture, and their commitment to cyber and adherence to security practices send a powerful message to employees. Leaders can demonstrate this commitment by actively participating in cyber awareness campaigns, championing security initiatives, and advocating for the necessary resources to implement and maintain an effective cyber strategy.

Leaders are also responsible for holding employees accountable for adhering to cyber policies and procedures. This can be achieved through clear communication of expectations, regular performance reviews, and consistent enforcement of consequences for non-compliance. At the same time, leaders should recognize and reward employees who demonstrate a strong commitment to cyber best practices, as this positive reinforcement can encourage others to follow suit.

Leading by example is crucial when it comes to cyber. Leaders should model good cyber habits, such as using strong passwords, practicing secure email and web browsing habits, and reporting suspicious activities. By consistently demonstrating these behaviors, leaders can help create a culture where cyber is seen as a shared responsibility and an integral part of everyone's job.

Finally, leaders should actively engage with their cyber teams and stay informed about the latest threats, trends, and best practices. This engagement can help ensure that cyber remains a top priority and that the organization is well-positioned to adapt to the ever-changing threat landscape.

Question 9: How can we leverage external partners to enhance our overall cyber posture?

Answer: Engaging with external partners is a collaborative approach that can provide valuable expertise and resources to enhance your organization's cyber posture. Managed Security Service Providers (MSSPs) offer various security services, including 24/7 monitoring, threat detection, incident response, and security information and event management (SIEM). By partnering with an MSSP, organizations can access advanced security technologies and a team of experienced security professionals without the need to build and maintain these capabilities in-house.

Collaborating with cyber vendors and solution providers can help organizations stay informed about the latest threats, technologies, and best practices. These vendors often have deep expertise in specific areas of cyber. They can provide valuable guidance on selecting and implementing the right security tools and strategies for your organization's unique needs and risk profile.

Participating in industry associations and forums is another way to leverage external partnerships. These groups bring together professionals from various organizations to share knowledge, experiences, and best practices related to cyber. By actively engaging in these communities, organizations can stay informed about emerging threats, learn from the successes and challenges of their peers, and contribute to the collective knowledge and advancement of the cyber field.

Finally, maintaining open lines of communication with law enforcement and regulatory agencies can be beneficial in a cyber attack or breach. These agencies can guide incident response, evidence preservation, and legal and regulatory compliance. Building relationships with these agencies before an incident can help streamline communication and coordination during a crisis.

By strategically leveraging these external partnerships, organizations can augment their internal capabilities, stay ahead of evolving threats, and build a more robust and resilient cyber posture.

Further Reading

1. Moeller, R. R. (2011). COSO enterprise risk management: Establishing effective governance, risk, and compliance processes (2nd ed.). Wiley.

2. Rios, B. (2021). Cyber risk management: Mastering the fundamentals using the NIST cyber framework (2nd ed.). Wiley.

3. Koontz, L. (2010). Best practices for implementing a security awareness program. SANS Institute. https://www.sans.org/reading-room/whitepapers/awareness/practices-implementing-security-awareness-program-33013

4. International Organization for Standardization & International Electrotechnical Commission. (2013). ISO/IEC 27001:2013 Information technology - Security techniques - Information security management systems - Requirements. https://www.iso.org/standard/54534.html

5. Fitzgerald, T., & Krause, M. (2008). CISO leadership: Essential principles for success. Auerbach Publications.

Chapter 4

Understanding The Complexity Of Cyber Law And Ethics

As businesses increasingly rely on digital technologies, cyber's legal and ethical implications have become more complex and consequential. This chapter explores cyber law and ethics intricacies, providing leaders with a foundational understanding of the legal landscape, an appreciation for the ethical boundaries in the digital realm, and strategies for leveraging compliance as a competitive advantage.

The Legal Landscape: What You Can't Afford to Ignore

Cyber law is a dynamic field, with regulations constantly evolving to keep pace with emerging technologies and threats. Data privacy laws, such as the General Data Protection Regulation (GDPR) in Europe and the California Consumer Privacy Act (CCPA) in the United States, dictate how organizations collect, store, and use personal information. Understanding and complying with these regulations is essential to avoid hefty fines and reputational damage.

For instance, under GDPR, organizations must have a lawful basis for collecting personal data, such as user consent or a legitimate business interest. Individuals have the right to access their data, request rectification of inaccuracies, and request erasure under certain circumstances. Organizations must also implement appropriate technical and organizational safeguards to protect personal data from unauthorized access, disclosure, alteration, or destruction.

Cyber laws, such as the Cyber Act (CSA) in Australia and the Gramm-Leach-Bliley Act (GLBA) in the United States, mandate specific security measures for organizations handling sensitive data. These laws outline requirements for data encryption, incident reporting, and risk management practices. Failing to comply with these regulations can result in legal repercussions.

The CSA, for example, outlines a framework for protecting critical infrastructure from cyber attacks. Critical infrastructure operators must identify and manage cyber risks, implement risk mitigation strategies, and report cyber incidents to relevant authorities. The GLBA, on the other hand, focuses on protecting the privacy and security of customer financial information held by financial institutions.

Intellectual property laws, including copyright, trademark, and patent laws, also apply in the digital space. Understanding these laws is crucial for protecting intellectual property and avoiding infringement on others' rights.

Copyright law protects original creative works such as software code, written content, and artistic designs. Trademarks protect distinctive words, symbols, or phrases used to identify the source of goods or services. Patents protect inventions, new processes, and improvements on existing inventions. Violating these laws can result in lawsuits, financial penalties, and potential cease-and-desist orders.

The legal landscape can vary depending on your location and industry. It's crucial to consult with local legal professionals to ensure your organization remains compliant with relevant cyber law regulations. They can guide specific regulations, data breach notification requirements, and international data transfer considerations.

Ethical Boundaries in a Digital World

The prevalence of digital technologies presents ethical dilemmas that traditional frameworks may not fully address. The tension between individual privacy and the need for security is a constant challenge. Strong security measures may involve collecting and analyzing data and raising privacy concerns. Balancing these competing interests requires careful consideration.

For instance, businesses may use cookies to track user behavior on their websites to personalize the user experience and display targeted advertising. However, this practice raises privacy concerns as it involves collecting user data without explicit consent. Organizations should implement clear cookie policies and allow users to control how their data is collected and used.

As AI becomes increasingly sophisticated, ethical questions regarding bias, transparency, and accountability arise. Organizations developing or utilizing AI must consider the ethical implications and implement safeguards to ensure fair and unbiased decision-making.

Bias in AI algorithms can stem from the data used to train them. If the training data reflects existing societal biases, the AI model may perpetuate those biases in its outputs. Organizations must ensure their AI development processes involve diverse data sets and implement fairness checks to identify and mitigate potential biases in AI decision-making.

Ethical considerations also arise when discovering cyber vulnerabilities. Should the vulnerability be disclosed publicly to raise awareness and allow for patching, or should it be kept private to prevent exploitation? Organizations must weigh the potential harm of disclosure against the risk of a cyber attack if the vulnerability remains unaddressed.

A responsible disclosure policy can help overcome this ethical dilemma. Such a policy outlines a process for reporting vulnerabilities to software vendors or relevant authorities while minimizing the window for attackers to exploit them. This policy promotes collaboration between security researchers and organizations to address vulnerabilities and improve the overall cyber posture.

The rise of cyber warfare raises complex legal and ethical questions. International law governing traditional warfare may not adequately address cyber attacks launched across borders, creating uncertainty regarding attribution, retaliation, and the legal implications of cyber operations. Developing international norms and frameworks for cyber warfare is an ongoing discussion within the global community.

Compliance as a Competitive Advantage

Compliance with cyber law and ethical practices goes beyond avoiding legal trouble; it can be a strategic advantage. Demonstrating a commitment to data privacy and ethical conduct fosters trust with customers, partners, and investors, improving relationships and brand loyalty.

Cyber breaches and unethical practices can have a devastating impact on an organization's reputation. Compliance helps protect your reputation and build confidence in your brand.

In some industries, compliance with specific cyber standards is required to participate in tenders or enter new markets. Demonstrating compliance can be a crucial differentiator when competing for these opportunities.

For instance, organizations in the healthcare industry may need to comply with regulations like HIPAA (Health Insurance Portability and Accountability Act) to protect patient data. Compliance with these regulations can be crucial for securing contracts with healthcare providers.

Strategies for Building a Culture of Cyber Law and Ethics

Fostering a culture of cyber law and ethics is an ongoing process that requires leadership commitment and employee engagement. Leaders set the tone for the organization's approach to cyber law and ethics, and their visible commitment to these principles sends a powerful message to employees.

It is crucial to regularly educate and train employees on cyber law, ethical considerations, and best practices in the digital realm. This training should raise awareness of relevant regulations, potential ethical dilemmas, and secure and responsible online behavior strategies.

Developing and implementing clear policies and procedures on data privacy, cyber, and acceptable use of technology is essential. These policies should be readily accessible to all employees and outline expectations for handling data, protecting information assets, and using company technology ethically.

Creating open communication channels where employees can raise concerns about potential legal or ethical issues without fear of reprisal is crucial. It encourages employees to report suspicious activity, seek guidance when faced with ethical dilemmas, and contribute to a culture of compliance.

Recognizing and rewarding employees who demonstrate ethical behavior and commitment to cyber best practices can further reinforce these principles and contribute to a more robust culture of compliance.

An internal (independent) audit team that monitors, assesses, and advises helps ensure compliance with policies and procedures.

Ethics across the Value Chain

Given the proliferation of cyber threat vectors in a company's supply chain and ecosystem, a key consideration is the level of ethical policy or guidelines we suggest or mandate across our value chain. Let's take a hypothetical large multinational retailer with a complex global supply chain spanning hundreds of suppliers and partners. To manage cyber risk across this ecosystem, the company could:

- Develop a comprehensive third-party risk management framework with clear cyber and data privacy standards that all suppliers must meet: this could involve requiring suppliers to complete detailed security questionnaires, submit to periodic audits, and maintain specific certifications (e.g., ISO 27001).

- Include specific cyber and data protection requirements in all supplier contracts and SLAs: this could cover incident notification procedures, data handling practices, and the right to terminate the relationship if security standards are unmet.

- Conduct regular risk assessments of the supply chain to identify weak links and concentrate oversight on the highest-risk suppliers (e.g., those handling the most sensitive data or providing the most critical services): this could involve on-site inspections, penetration testing, or a review of supplier security documentation and incident logs.

- Provide cyber training and resources to help suppliers improve their practices: this could include secure coding workshops for software providers, data handling guidelines for logistics partners, or subsidized access to security tools and monitoring services.

- Participate in industry information-sharing groups and collaborate with peer organizations to collectively monitor and mitigate supply chain threats: This could involve sharing threat intelligence, conducting joint vulnerability assessments, or coordinating incident response planning for shared suppliers.

An example of Ethical Decision Making

Leaders must understand the flow and process of ethical

decision-making in a cyber context. To that end, we have created an example of a generic healthcare provider.

The healthcare provider is developing an AI system to help triage patients and recommend treatments. The system will be trained on a large dataset of patient records, including sensitive information about medical conditions, treatments, and outcomes.

In designing and deploying this system, the organization would need to consider various ethical implications and make decisions informed by core principles of medical ethics (beneficence, non-maleficence, autonomy, and justice). For example:

- *Beneficence (doing good):* The AI system has the potential to improve patient outcomes by helping doctors make faster, more accurate diagnoses and treatment decisions. However, the organization would need to ensure the system is rigorously tested for safety and efficacy before deployment and continuously monitored for unintended consequences or errors that could harm patients.

- *Non-maleficence (avoiding harm):* The sensitive patient data used to train the AI system could be highly damaging if leaked or misused. The organization would need to implement strict data security and access controls, ensuring only authorized personnel can access the data and that it is not used for any purposes beyond the legitimate scope of the AI project.

- *Autonomy (respecting individual rights and choices):* Patients may be concerned about their medical information being used to train an AI system without their knowledge or consent. The organization would need to develop clear data governance policies and engage in proactive patient communication and consent management to ensure individuals understand how their data may be used and have the opportunity to opt-out if desired.

- *Justice (promoting fairness and equity):* If the patient data used to train the AI system does not represent the broader population (e.g., skewing toward specific demographics), the resulting system could produce biased or discriminatory recommendations. The organization would need to carefully audit training data for diversity and fairness and test the system for equitable performance across different patient populations.

To make this system effective, ongoing collaboration between the organization's medical, technical, legal, and ethics experts would be required to ensure the AI system is developed and deployed consistently with core values and regulatory requirements. Key decision points, risks, and mitigation strategies must be carefully documented and revisited over time as the system evolves and new ethical challenges emerge.

Conclusion

Understanding the complexities of cyber law and ethics is essential for any organization operating in the digital realm. Staying informed about evolving legal regulations, understanding ethical dilemmas, and leveraging compliance as a competitive advantage are crucial to building a secure and responsible digital presence. By prioritizing these considerations and implementing effective strategies, you can foster trust, mitigate risks, and ensure your organization thrives in the digital age. While the Ethics of Cyber is a book topic in its own right, the critical thing for you to consider is your ethical/legal stance and ensure that you are feeding that into your discussions on Cyber as a strategic business priority. Ethics is not something that should be applied "after the fact." It needs to be a key input for your discussion.

Answers To Key Questions

Question 1: What are the most critical legal and regulatory cyber requirements that affect our operations?

Answer: Identifying the most critical legal and regulatory requirements depends on your industry, location, and the type of data you handle. However, some common areas to consider include data privacy, cyber, and intellectual property laws.

Data privacy laws, such as GDPR and CCPA, likely require obtaining user consent, implementing data security measures, and providing individuals with the right to access, rectify, or erase their data. Cyber laws, like the CSA or GLBA, may dictate specific security controls you must implement, such as data encryption, access controls, and incident reporting procedures. Intellectual property laws also apply to digital assets, so ensure you have the proper licenses for the software you use and respect the intellectual property rights of others.

Conducting a legal compliance audit can help identify specific regulations applicable to your organization. Partnering with legal counsel ensures you stay updated on the evolving legal landscape and prioritize the most critical requirements impacting your operations.

Question 2: How do we enforce ethical practices in the use of digital technologies across our business?

Answer: Enforcing ethical practices requires a multi-pronged approach. A good starting point is to develop a clear code of ethics outlining your organization's commitment to ethical behavior in the digital realm. This code should address issues like data privacy, intellectual property, online conduct, and responsible use of technology.

Training employees on the code of ethics and integrating discussions on ethical dilemmas into training programs is crucial. Simulations and case studies can help employees understand how digital technologies can pose ethical challenges. Leadership commitment also plays a vital role in setting the tone. Active leadership in promoting ethical practices demonstrates their importance and encourages employees to follow suit.

Establishing clear channels for employees to report suspected unethical behavior or potential legal violations is essential. Investigate reports thoroughly and take appropriate corrective actions to deter future misconduct. Using an internal (independent) audit team to monitor, assess, and advise is helpful to ensure compliance with policies and procedures.

By implementing these steps, you can create a culture of accountability and encourage ethical decision-making within your organization.

Question 3: In what ways are we leveraging compliance to gain a competitive edge?

Answer: Compliance with cyber law and ethical practices can offer several competitive advantages. Demonstrating compliance fosters trust and loyalty among customers, leading to improved customer relationships. Customers are increasingly concerned about data privacy and security, so organizations prioritizing these aspects can stand out from competitors.

Compliance also reduces the risk of legal penalties, reputational damage, and costly cyber attacks. This translates to a more stable and secure business environment that can attract potential customers, partners, and investors. Certain industries and government contracts require compliance with specific cyber standards. Demonstrating compliance can be a crucial differentiator when competing for these opportunities.

Furthermore, a commitment to ethical conduct and data privacy enhances your brand image and attracts talent and partners who value these principles. Compliance goes beyond avoiding legal trouble. It signifies your organization's commitment to responsible data practices and operating with integrity, which can be a powerful differentiator in today's competitive landscape.

Question 4: How do we stay updated with the rapidly changing landscape of cyber law?

Answer: The cyber law landscape constantly evolves, but several ways exist to stay informed. Industry newsletters, legal publications, and relevant government agency websites can provide updates on regulatory changes. Attending industry events and conferences offers opportunities to hear from legal experts and network with other professionals facing similar challenges.

Partnering with experienced legal counsel ensures you receive expert advice on navigating complex legal issues and interpreting evolving regulations. Establishing internal processes for monitoring legal developments is also important. This could involve assigning someone to research changes or implementing automated alerts for relevant regulatory updates.

It is crucial to have dedicated resources responsible for tracking legal developments and disseminating critical updates to relevant stakeholders within your organization. This helps ensure your cyber practices and policies comply with the latest legal requirements.

Question 5: How are we ensuring that our third-party vendors comply with our cyber standards?

Answer: Reliance on third-party vendors introduces additional security risks, so ensuring their compliance in cyber security protocols is crucial. A good starting point is to include clear cyber clauses in vendor contracts that outline specific security requirements, data handling practices, and breach notification procedures.

Conduct thorough due diligence on potential vendors. Assess their cyber posture, data security practices, and history of security incidents. Reserving the right to perform security audits or request vendor assessments can help verify their compliance with your cyber standards.

Continuously monitoring vendor activity and their access to your systems is also crucial. Look for suspicious activity and ensure they are adhering to contractual agreements. Regularly review and update vendor agreements to reflect changes in your cyber requirements or the vendor's services.

Establishing a vendor risk management program can help formalize the process of assessing, monitoring, and mitigating risks associated with third-party vendors. This program should include clear policies and procedures for onboarding new vendors, conducting periodic risk assessments, and managing vendor relationships throughout the lifecycle of the engagement.

Question 6: What systems do we have in place to handle ethical dilemmas arising from digital data usage?

Answer: Ethical dilemmas in the digital realm require thoughtful consideration. Forming an internal ethics committee with diverse perspectives to review and offer guidance on potential ethical dilemmas related to data usage can be helpful.

Developing a decision-making framework that outlines critical ethical principles and considerations when making decisions about data collection, storage, and use can guide employees. Training employees on the framework and equipping them with tools and resources to identify and address potential ethical concerns is essential.

Encouraging open communication where employees feel comfortable raising concerns about ethical dilemmas without fear of reprisal can help surface potential issues early on. Establishing clear escalation pathways for ethical concerns and ensuring that senior leadership is involved in addressing significant ethical dilemmas is crucial.

Regularly reviewing and auditing data practices can help identify potential ethical risks and ensure that data is being used consistently with your organization's values and principles. Engaging external experts, such as ethicists or privacy advocates, can provide valuable perspectives and guidance on navigating complex ethical issues.

Question 7: How do we integrate cyber law and ethics into our training programs?

Answer: Cyber law and ethics training are crucial for building a secure and responsible workforce. Developing training programs specific to different employee roles and responsibilities is essential. Executives may need a broader awareness of legal and ethical considerations, while technical teams might benefit from in-depth training on security protocols.

Incorporating interactive learning methods like case studies, simulations, and role-playing exercises can make learning engaging and help employees apply concepts to real-world situations. Conducting regular training sessions ensures employees stay current on evolving legal regulations and ethical considerations in the digital realm.

Launching ongoing awareness campaigns through internal communication channels can keep cyber and ethics top-of-mind for all employees. Integrating cyber law and ethics content into new employee onboarding and annual compliance training ensures that all employees have a foundational understanding of these critical issues.

Measuring the effectiveness of training programs through assessments, surveys, and tracking employee behavior can help identify areas for improvement and demonstrate the impact of your training efforts. Regularly updating training content to reflect changes in laws, regulations, and ethical best practices is essential to keep your workforce informed and prepared.

Question 8: How does our cyber compliance affect our international operations?

Answer: Cyber regulations vary across countries, so when operating internationally, you must identify and understand the cyber regulations applicable to each country where you operate. This may require collaborating with local legal counsel.

While striving for consistency in your security posture, consider local laws and regulations when implementing security controls. Balancing standardization with localization is critical. Regulations like GDPR may restrict data transfers outside the European Economic Area (EEA), so developing clear data transfer procedures that comply with relevant laws is essential.

It is crucial to conduct a thorough assessment of your international operations to identify potential compliance gaps and develop a plan to address them. This may involve implementing additional security measures, updating policies and procedures, or investing in local infrastructure to ensure compliance with local regulations.

Cyber threats are global, so it is essential to collaborate with international law enforcement or cyber agencies, if necessary, to address a cyber attack or investigate a breach. Establishing relationships with local authorities and understanding their expectations and protocols can help streamline incident response and investigations.

It is essential to regularly monitor and audit your international operations for compliance with local regulations and your organization's global cyber standards. This can help identify potential issues early on and ensure your organization maintains a strong cyber posture.

Question 9: Are we prepared for the legal implications of a potential cyber breach?

Answer: Cyber breaches can have significant legal ramifications, so ensuring preparedness is crucial. Developing a comprehensive incident response plan that outlines procedures for detecting, responding to, and recovering from a cyber attack is essential.

Understanding your obligations under data breach notification laws in the jurisdictions you operate in is also crucial. These laws typically dictate timelines for notifying affected individuals and relevant authorities in case of a breach. Failure to comply with these requirements can result in significant legal penalties and reputational damage.

Engaging with legal counsel to understand your organization's specific legal obligations and liabilities in the event of a breach is essential. This includes understanding potential legal defenses, insurance coverage, and strategies for minimizing legal exposure.

Regular tabletop exercises and simulations can help test your incident response plan and identify potential gaps or weaknesses. These exercises should involve stakeholders across the organization, including legal, IT, and communications teams.

Following a breach, conducting a thorough post-incident review is crucial to identify root causes, implement corrective actions, and prevent similar incidents from occurring in the future. This post-incident review can help strengthen your cyber posture and demonstrate a commitment to continuous improvement.

By proactively preparing for the legal implications of a potential cyber breach, you can minimize the impact of an incident and ensure that your organization is well-positioned to respond and recover effectively.

Further Reading

1. Samuelson, P. (2016). Intellectual property and the digital economy: Why the anti-circumvention regulations must be revised. Berkeley Technology Law Journal, 14(2), 519-566. https://doi.org/10.15779/Z38DD0R

2. Solove, D. J., & Schwartz, P. M. (2017). Information privacy law (6th ed.). Wolters Kluwer.

3. Lessig, L. (2006). Code: Version 2.0. Basic Books.

4. Lin, P., Abney, K., & Bekey, G. A. (Eds.). (2012). Robot ethics: The ethical and social implications of robotics. The MIT Press.

5. European Parliament and Council of the European Union. (2016). Regulation (EU) 2016/679 of the European Parliament and of the Council of 27 April 2016 on protecting natural persons about the processing of personal data and on the free movement of such data, and repealing Directive 95/46/EC (General Data Protection Regulation). Official Journal of the European Union, L119, 1-88. http://data.europa.eu/eli/reg/2016/679/oj

Chapter 5

Leading Cyber Culture From The C-Suite

Cyber security has become a critical concern for organizations of all sizes. As cyber threats evolve and become more sophisticated, leaders must actively create and maintain a robust cyber culture within their organizations. This chapter will explore the essential steps all Leaders and senior executives can take to lead by example and foster a cyber security culture permeating every level of the organization.

Setting the Tone at the Top

The foundation of a robust cyber culture begins with the organization's leadership. C-suite executives and senior leaders must demonstrate a personal commitment to cyber security and communicate its importance to the entire organization. By aligning cyber security with business objectives, leaders can ensure that it is not viewed as a mere technical issue but a critical component of the organization's overall strategy.

One powerful example of setting the tone at the top comes from the CEO of JPMorgan Chase, Jamie Dimon. In his annual letter to shareholders, Dimon consistently emphasizes the importance of cyber security and the bank's ongoing efforts to strengthen its defenses. He states, "Cyber security is a top priority for us, and we continue to invest heavily in improving our cyber defenses and enhancing our resilience". By openly communicating the bank's commitment to cyber security, Dimon sends a clear message to employees, customers, and shareholders that it is a critical priority for the organization.

Leaders must also encourage open communication and transparency about cyber risks. Leaders can foster a culture of vigilance and proactivity by creating an environment where employees feel comfortable reporting potential threats or vulnerabilities. The leadership at Lockheed Martin, a global aerospace and defense company, exemplifies this approach. The company's CEO, James Taiclet, emphasizes the importance of open communication and encourages employees to report any suspicious activity, stating, "We need everyone's help to keep our networks and our business secure. If you see something, say something". By promoting a culture of transparency and encouraging employee involvement, Lockheed Martin's leadership demonstrates its commitment to cyber.

Establishing Clear Policies and Procedures

Organizations must have comprehensive cyber security policies in place to effectively lead a cyber culture. These policies should be easily accessible and understandable to all employees, regardless of their technical expertise. Regular review and updates are essential to ensure policies keep pace with evolving threats and industry best practices.

One organization that has successfully implemented clear cyber security policies is the National Institute of Standards and Technology (NIST). NIST's Cyber Security Framework provides guidelines and best practices for organizations to manage and reduce cyber risks (NIST, 2021). The framework is designed to be flexible and adaptable to each organization's unique needs, making it a valuable resource for leaders looking to establish effective cyber security policies.

Equally important is the consistent and fair enforcement of these policies. Leaders must ensure that all employees, regardless of their position or seniority, are held accountable for adhering to cyber security protocols. A notable example of this is the case of a former Coca-Cola employee sentenced to prison for stealing trade secrets and attempting to sell them to a competitor. The company's swift action in reporting the incident to authorities and cooperating with the investigation demonstrates its commitment to enforcing its cyber security policies and holding employees accountable for their actions.

Investing in Cyber security Education and Training

To create a robust cyber culture, organizations must invest in the education and training of their employees. Regular cyber security training should be provided to all employees, with content tailored to their specific roles and responsibilities. Leaders should also encourage continuous learning and skill development to ensure employees stay up-to-date with the latest threats and best practices.

IBM is one company that has made significant investments in cyber security education. The company's Security Education and Training program offers employees a wide range of courses and certifications, covering topics such as secure coding, incident response, and risk management. By providing comprehensive training and encouraging continuous learning, IBM equips its workforce with the knowledge and skills needed to maintain a robust cyber culture.

Leaders must also lead by example and actively participate in cyber security training. This demonstrates to employees that cyber security is a priority for the organization and that everyone, including senior executives, has a role to play in maintaining a secure environment. A powerful example is the "Hacker in Chief" Initiative launched by Shridhar Mittal, CEO of mobile security firm Zimperium. Mittal encourages fellow CEOs to experience a firsthand simulated cyberattack to understand better their organizations' risks and challenges.

Fostering a Culture of Collaboration and Accountability

To effectively lead a cyber culture, organizations must foster a culture of collaboration and accountability. This involves promoting cross-functional collaboration between IT, security, and business units to ensure that cyber security is integrated into all aspects of the organization's operations. By breaking down silos and encouraging open communication, leaders can create a more cohesive and effective approach to cyber security.

Microsoft's approach is an excellent example of fostering collaboration and accountability. The company has established a "Digital Diplomacy" team that brings together experts from across the organization, including legal, policy, and technical professionals, to address cyber security challenges. Microsoft can develop more comprehensive and effective solutions to complex cyber security issues by promoting cross-functional collaboration.

Leaders must also empower employees to take ownership of cyber security and recognize and reward positive behaviors. This can include acknowledging employees reporting potential threats or vulnerabilities or celebrating teams demonstrating exceptional cyber security practices. By creating a culture where cyber security is everyone's responsibility, leaders can foster a sense of accountability and engagement throughout the organization.

A great example of this approach is Siemens's "Cyber Heroes" program. The program recognizes employees who go above and beyond to promote cyber security, such as identifying and reporting potential threats or developing innovative security solutions. By celebrating these "Cyber Heroes," Siemens reinforces the importance of cyber security and actively encourages all employees to maintain a secure environment.

Communicating Cyber Priorities to Stakeholders

Effective communication is critical for building and maintaining a robust cyber culture. Executives must communicate cyber priorities to stakeholders, including the Board of Directors, investors and shareholders, and customers and partners.

It is essential to regularly update the Board on the organization's cyber posture, including risks, mitigation strategies, and the security program's overall effectiveness. Cyber metrics and reports should be presented concisely and relevantly to facilitate the Board's understanding.

Communicating the organization's commitment to cyber and its impact on long-term business sustainability and shareholder value is essential for investors and shareholders. Highlighting how a strong security posture can mitigate risks, protect customer data, and build investor trust can demonstrate the value of cyber investments.

Being transparent about cyber practices and demonstrating a commitment to protecting customer and partner data is crucial. Implementing a security awareness program for customers and partners, publishing security white papers, conducting joint security workshops, or clearly describing how the organization handles customer data breaches can help build trust and transparency with stakeholders, creating a more robust cyber ecosystem.

Conclusion:

Creating and maintaining a robust cyber culture is a critical responsibility for today's C-suite leaders. Leaders can effectively navigate cyber security's complex and ever-evolving landscape by setting the tone at the top, establishing clear policies and procedures, investing in education and training, and fostering a culture of collaboration and accountability.

The examples provided throughout this chapter demonstrate the impact of effective leadership on an organization's cyber culture. From Jamie Dimon's consistent emphasis on cyber security at JPMorgan Chase to Microsoft's cross-functional "Digital Diplomacy" team, these real-world cases illustrate the power of leadership in driving positive change and creating a more secure environment.

As cyber threats continue to evolve and become more sophisticated, the role of leadership in maintaining a robust cyber culture will only become more critical. By taking a proactive and engaged approach to cyber security, C-suite executives can protect their organizations from potential threats and create a competitive advantage in an increasingly digital world. The benefits of a robust cyber culture are clear – from reduced risk and improved resilience to increased customer trust and loyalty.

In conclusion, leading a cyber culture from the C-suite is not a one-time initiative but an ongoing commitment that requires consistent effort and attention. By embracing their role as cyber security leaders and taking meaningful action to promote a security culture, C-suite executives can position their organizations for success in the face of ever-evolving cyber threats.

Answers To Key Questions

Question 1: What initiatives are organizations taking to cultivate a security-first mindset among all employees?

Answer: Cultivating a security-first mindset among all employees requires a multifaceted approach. Regular security awareness training sessions are crucial to updating employees on the latest cyber threats, emphasizing best practices like maintaining strong passwords, identifying phishing attempts, and ensuring everyone knows the correct procedures for reporting suspicious activity.

Organizations should go beyond simple lectures to make training effective and use interactive modules, gamification, and realistic scenarios to make security relevant to specific job roles.

Leadership plays a vital role in awareness campaigns. When senior figures actively participate, it underscores the importance of security across all company levels. Positive reinforcement is also crucial---employees who demonstrate strong security habits, whether reporting a suspicious email or offering a constructive security suggestion, should receive recognition for their actions.

Question 2: How can leadership demonstrate commitment to cyber?

Answer: Leadership teams can demonstrate their commitment to cyber in several ways. They should prioritize cyber by publicly advocating for it in company-wide communications, boardroom discussions, and external interactions. This commitment must be backed up with resources, including investments in robust security tools, comprehensive training programs, and dedicated security professionals.

Furthermore, leadership must understand that cyber isn't a separate issue from normal business; it's woven into the company's fabric. They should ensure security considerations are always included in strategic planning, guaranteeing that security measures support and enable business objectives. Perhaps most importantly, leaders must practice what they preach. They should exhibit vital security behaviors by using complex passwords, exercising caution online, and strictly following data security protocols. This sets a powerful example for the entire organization. These initiatives should be led by an executive board-level champion, supported by a suitably qualified non-executive director (or equivalent) to provide focus.

Question 3: How can organizations integrate cyber into their core business functions?

Answer: To effectively integrate cyber into core business functions, organizations should view security as an integral part of the business, not an add-on consideration. This means embedding security into several key areas. First, security reviews should be conducted at all stages of business processes---whether developing new software, choosing vendors, managing the supply chain, or running marketing campaigns. This proactive approach allows organizations to identify and address potential vulnerabilities before they become problems.

Strong collaboration between the security team and other departments should also be prioritized. Open communication ensures that security expertise is always accessible, making the cyber approach more comprehensive and practical. Finally, organizations may explore the concept of "security champions"---individuals within different departments who promote security awareness and best practices among their colleagues.

Question 4: How should organizations communicate the importance of cyber to all stakeholders?

Answer: Clear and tailored communication is critical to building a company-wide understanding of cyber risks and establishing trust. The approach to communicating with stakeholders should vary depending on their unique needs and interests.

For the Board of Directors, organizations should provide regular, in-depth cyber reports that focus on strategic implications. Technical jargon should be avoided, presenting the Board with a clear picture of potential risks, the progress of mitigation plans, and a comprehensive assessment of the security posture. With investors and shareholders, communication should emphasize the direct connection between robust cyber and the long-term health and stability of the company, assuring them that the protection of their investment is taken exceptionally seriously.

Building trust with customers and partners hinges on transparency. Organizations can demonstrate their commitment to data protection in multiple ways, such as publishing detailed security white papers that outline their practices, offering collaborative security workshops to discuss shared concerns, or providing easily accessible, plain-language information about their breach response protocols.

Question 5: What key cyber behaviors should be expected from the leadership team?

Answer: The leadership team sets the standard for cyber behavior within an organization. They should be vocal cyber champions, constantly reinforcing its importance through their words and actions. Most importantly, they must personally embody the secure behaviors they advocate---utilizing strong passwords, handling data carefully, and always maintaining a critical eye toward potential threats.

Data and analysis are essential tools for leaders, guiding security decisions based on informed risk assessments. Furthermore, leaders must hold themselves and their teams accountable for robust cyber practices. This means actively fostering security awareness and ensuring everyone under their supervision understands and follows the organization's policies. Finally, in the ever-evolving world of cyber, leaders must demonstrate a commitment to continuous learning, always staying updated on the latest threats and best practices to protect the organization.

Question 6: How can organizations ensure cyber is a regular topic at Board meetings?

Answer: Organizations should take several steps to ensure cyber remains a priority on the Board's agenda. First, an executive board-level champion should lead the cyber agenda, supported by a suitably qualified non-executive director (or equivalent) to provide focus.

Regular security briefings should be scheduled once this leadership is in place as a standing item during Board meetings. These briefings give the Board an up-to-date picture of the threat landscape, the progress of ongoing security projects, and details of any recent security incidents.

Additionally, organizations should provide the Board with meaningful security metrics. These metrics track the health of the security program and might include the number of vulnerabilities fixed, the number of employees who fall for phishing simulations, or the number of security incidents logged. By presenting data in this way, the Board is given a tangible way to measure progress and identify areas for improvement.

Finally, investing in cyber awareness training explicitly designed for Board members is essential. These sessions help them better understand cyber's unique challenges, empowering them to make informed strategic decisions about security investments and policies.

Question 7: What approach should organizations take to balance openness and security in corporate culture?

Answer: Finding the right balance between openness and security is an ongoing challenge that organizations must take seriously. The principle of least privilege is a good starting point, meaning employees are given access to only the specific information and systems they genuinely need to perform their roles. This limits the potential fallout should a security breach occur. Additionally, data should be classified according to sensitivity, ensuring the most critical information receives the most stringent protection.

While these technical measures are crucial, technology alone isn't enough. Organizations should provide secure channels for communication and collaboration, striking a balance between open teamwork and necessary monitoring for potential threats. Perhaps most importantly, they should strive to create a company culture where employees feel empowered and encouraged to report suspicious activity or security concerns without fear of negative consequences. This open reporting allows organizations to avoid problems and create a secure environment.

Question 8: How can organizations maintain a dynamic and responsive cyber culture as they grow?

Answer: Maintaining a robust cyber culture as an organization grows means embracing change and staying ahead of the curve. This can be done in several ways. First, regular security assessments are essential. As the company expands, so does the potential attack surface---these assessments help find and address new vulnerabilities. Second, organizations should prioritize investing in security solutions designed to scale seamlessly alongside their growth. This might mean choosing cloud-based platforms or solutions with a modular design.

Furthermore, security awareness training can't be a one-time event. Organizations must continually update their training materials to reflect new threats and ensure they're relevant to the challenges of a growing company. Finally, organizations may need to bolster their security team as operations expand. Having the right expertise and resources in place ensures a strong security posture is maintained even during periods of rapid growth.

Question 9: What incentives can organizations use to encourage proactive cyber practices among employees?

Answer: Incentives can be a powerful tool for encouraging proactive cyber behaviors and creating a culture where security is everyone's concern. Instead of simply telling employees what to do, organizations should try to make security a rewarding experience. This means publicly celebrating employees who go the extra mile to protect systems, whether they've astutely spotted a phishing attempt or developed an innovative security solution. These rewards don't always need to be monetary; sometimes, company-wide recognition or small tokens of appreciation can be just as motivating.

Additionally, security training shouldn't be boring. Organizations can introduce gamification and friendly competition elements to make learning more engaging and rewarding. Finally, investing in employees' professional growth is crucial in supporting those who wish to deepen their cyber expertise. Offering opportunities like attending conferences or specialized training programs shows a commitment to the team and signals that cyber knowledge is a valuable path for career advancement within the company.

Further Reading

1. Kotter, J. P. (2012). Leading change. Harvard Business Review Press.

2. Schein, E. H. (2010). Organizational culture and leadership (4th ed.). Jossey-Bass.

3. Drucker, P. F. (2006). The effective executive: The definitive guide to getting the right things done. HarperCollins Publishers.

4. Goleman, D., Boyatzis, R., & McKee, A. (2013). Primal leadership: Unleashing the power of emotional intelligence. Harvard Business Review Press.

5. Covey, S. R. (2004). The 7 habits of highly effective people: Powerful lessons in personal change. Free Press.

Chapter 6

Cyber As An Investment, Not An Expense

Treating cyber as optional is a recipe for disaster in the business world. Businesses of all sizes are under constant attack, and the costs of a breach go far beyond the immediate financial hit. Lost revenue, shattered customer trust, legal fines - it's a cascade of damage that can cripple or even destroy a company. It's time to change our mindset: cyber isn't a cost; it's an investment in your company's survival and long-term success.

The True Cost of Cyber Ignorance

Too many companies try to minimize security spending, but the reality is that the cost of 'doing nothing' can be catastrophic. A cyber attack has two sides: the immediate fallout and the long-lasting scars.

First, there's the direct cost - the money you spend to contain the breach, notify customers, clean up the mess, and maybe even pay a ransom if your data is held hostage. But the long-term consequences can be even more devastating. If reputation takes a hit, rebuilding customer trust can be slow and expensive. Regulators might slap you with hefty fines, especially if your security is negligent. And even if nothing that dramatic happens, the fear of a breach erodes employee morale - who wants to work for a company that doesn't protect them?

Let's put some reality behind this. Think back to the Equifax breach a few years ago - their costs soared into the billions, and they're still struggling reputationally years later. Or remember the WannaCry ransomware attack that paralyzed businesses worldwide, causing losses across industries. These aren't isolated incidents. They illustrate the question every business must ask: Can you afford to be the next headline?

Measuring the Immeasurable: Cyber ROI

There's no denying that quantifying the exact return on investment (ROI) for security is challenging. You're paying to prevent something that might never happen! But that doesn't mean it is not a worthwhile investment. Here are some ways to make the value tangible.

Start with a cost-benefit analysis. It may not give an exact percentage, but it paints a stark picture. Estimate the costs of a significant breach, considering those factors we discussed, and compare that to the cost of implementing more robust security. This clarifies that spending a little now saves you a fortune later.

Next, do some threat modeling. Don't try to protect against everything - focus on the most likely attacks your industry faces. Research the financial hit for each of these. Then, you can prioritize your security spending to target those high-risk areas first, which maximizes impact per dollar spent.

Finally, think about "Return on Security Investment" (RoSI). This highlights the losses that good security prevents. So, if a new system decreases your risk of a ransomware attack that might cost a million dollars, that's a large chunk of your ROI. Of course, some of this involves estimation, but even a ballpark figure helps justify your spending.

Beyond the Numbers

Numbers matter, but they don't capture cyber's total value. Think about the less obvious ways a secure company is a stronger company:

- *Business as usual:* Good security minimizes downtime. A cyber attack can cripple your systems, but robust defenses keep you running rather than scrambling to recover and losing precious days of revenue.

- *Customer confidence:* In the digital age, customers are savvier about their data and choose companies that protect it. Being known for strong security is an intangible but powerful form of marketing. This translates directly to better customer loyalty and opens new markets.

- *Competitive edge:* Customers and partners flock to businesses that take security seriously. You might even win contracts simply because your security protocols are tighter than the other guys'!

- *Peace of mind:* Breaches aren't just a financial drain; they're stressful. Knowing you are protected boosts morale and keeps your team focused on productivity because they're not constantly fearing the next digital disaster.

Building a Business Case for Cyber Spending

Getting the funds for robust security means more than just reciting scary statistics. You need a tailored business case that speaks the language of the people signing the checks.

Of course, making a compelling case for cyber in resource-constrained environments or tough economic times is even more complex. Even during challenging economic periods, cyber must remain a top priority. While cutting security budgets to save costs may be tempting, the potential consequences of a breach - financial losses, reputational damage, and legal liabilities - far outweigh any short-term savings.

Let's create a hypothetical case. You are a mid-sized retailer facing budget pressure due to an economic downturn. By carefully assessing your security priorities, your company identifies that protecting its e-commerce platform and customer data is paramount, as a breach could be catastrophic to its online revenue.

The CISO makes the case to maintain funding for critical e-commerce security measures like regular penetration testing, web application firewalls, and customer authentication systems. They also propose cost-saving measures like consolidating security tools and renegotiating vendor contracts to optimize spend.

By framing the focused investments as essential to protecting the company's core business and presenting a precise cost-benefit analysis, the Chief Information Security Officer (CISO) secures leadership buy-in to prioritize e-commerce security despite the constraining budget environment.

First, connect security to the big picture. If you pitch to the CEO, emphasize how this protects the core operations, the R&D that will lead to your next big product or the customer data that drives long-term growth. Cyber isn't some isolated IT expense; it enables the broader business to succeed. Here is a process you can follow to help you get the buy-in from your senior colleagues:

- ***Quantify the risks:*** Use industry data and your company's metrics to estimate the potential cost of a security incident. This might include direct expenses like investigation and remediation and indirect costs like lost business and decreased shareholder value. Comparing these figures to the cost of maintaining robust security can help justify the investment.

- Pri***oritize based on impact:*** Focus resources on protecting your most critical assets and mitigating your highest-likelihood threats. Conducting a thorough risk assessment can help identify these priorities.

- ***Look for efficiencies:*** Explore ways to optimize your security investments before cutting them. This could involve renegotiating vendor contracts, consolidating tools, or automating manual processes to free up your security team's time.

- ***Leverage shared services:*** Consider partnering with other organizations to share the cost of certain security functions, like threat intelligence or incident response. Managed security service providers (MSSPs) can also provide expert capabilities at a predictable cost.
- ***Frame security as a business enabler:*** Highlight how strong security can help achieve business goals even in lean times, such as enabling safe remote work to maintain productivity or providing the assurance to enter new markets and revenue streams.

Wherever you can, tie spending requests to ROI. Use the methods we discussed - cost avoidance and potential new revenue. Even estimates speak louder than vague pleas for money. And remember, tailor your pitch! A presentation for marketing should highlight the customer trust angle, while for the tech team, focus on operational efficiency and preventing those panicked calls for help after an attack.

Building this case takes work, but the payoff is immense. Think of it like insurance - the best outcome is not needing to use it but being prepared if the worst does happen.

The Human Element: Building a Culture of Cyber Awareness

You can buy all the fancy tech in the world, but you're still vulnerable if your employees don't understand the threats. That's why fostering a security-aware culture across the company is vital.

Picture it - many attacks succeed because someone clicked a bad link or fell for a convincing phishing email. Those mistakes are far less likely if you empower your employees with knowledge. Plus, if they understand what a potential attack looks like, they're more likely to speak up fast. Early reporting can often stop a breach before it becomes serious!

This means making security a shared responsibility, not just another IT chore. Here's how to make this culture shift happen:

- ***Training that sticks:*** Ditch those boring slideshows! Interactive sessions, quizzes, and even some simulated phishing attacks to get the adrenaline pumping help the lessons sink in. Use industry-specific examples to make the training relatable.

- ***Your security ambassadors:*** Find the naturally cyber-savvy folks in each department and get them on board. They can spread the word in a way policies and IT memos never will and answer colleagues' questions on a more personal level.

- ***Constant reminders:*** Don't just train and forget. Posters and security tips in newsletters... keep it top-of-mind so good habits become second nature. Weave security into the fabric of your company culture.

- ***Walk the walk:*** Leaders who treat passwords carelessly send the message that security isn't that important. Actions speak louder than any policy manual, so make sure leadership sets the right example.

- ***It's a win-win:*** A cyber-savvy workforce isn't just safer. It also leads to smoother operations (fewer accidental data leaks), better morale (who wants to feel like a target?), and faster incident response if something does happen. Investing in employee awareness is an investment in the smooth functioning of your entire business.

Evaluating and selecting security solutions

When evaluating security solutions, you must find the ones that deliver the best value. Cost is a crucial factor, but leaders must also consider a range of other criteria to ensure they're getting the best overall value for their investment.

Let's create another illustrative scenario. Your company wants to implement a new endpoint detection and response (EDR) solution. After assessing its risks, the company determines that the EDR tool must effectively detect and investigate threats across a complex environment of 10,000 endpoints, including a mix of on-premises and cloud workloads.

The security team evaluates several leading EDR solutions, considering factors like threat detection efficacy (based on third-party test results), ease of deployment and use, integration with their existing SIEM platform, and scalability to accommodate projected growth.

They narrowed it to two finalists and invited each vendor to conduct a proof-of-concept in their environment. Through this process, they found that while one solution has a lower upfront license cost, the other is easier to deploy, provides more intuitive investigation workflows, and includes access to a managed threat-hunting service - ultimately providing better total value.

By taking a holistic, value-driven approach to evaluation rather than just selecting the cheapest option, the company chooses an EDR solution to provide adequate, efficient protection for its specific environment and needs.

Some key factors to consider include:

- ***Alignment with risk priorities:*** Based on your risk assessment, the solution should address the threats and vulnerabilities most critical to your organization.

- ***Effectiveness:*** Look for solutions with a proven track record of preventing, detecting, and responding to real-world threats. This could be demonstrated through independent testing, customer references, or proof-of-concept trials.

- ***Ease of use and implementation:*** Complex tools that require extensive customization or specialized skills can lead to configuration errors and low adoption. Favor solutions that will be intuitive for your team to deploy, configure, and maintain.

- *Integration:* Consider how well the solution integrates with your existing security stack and IT environment. Tools that can seamlessly exchange data and coordinate with other systems will provide more efficient and effective protection.

- *Scalability:* Choose solutions that can grow with your organization and adapt to changing needs. This includes technical scalability (e.g., handling increasing volumes of data or users) and licensing flexibility.

- *Vendor support:* The quality and responsiveness of vendor support can be critical, especially during a live incident. Look for providers with strong SLAs, available training, and value-added services like threat hunting or incident response.

- *Total cost of ownership:* In addition to upfront costs, consider ongoing expenses like maintenance, support, and training over the solution's entire lifecycle. Also, factor in any cost savings the tool may provide by improving efficiency or reducing your team's workload.

Conclusion

Cyber investment may be a tough sell sometimes, but it's as essential as having a roof over your head. A proactive approach and building a culture of security awareness across your workforce are your best defenses against the ever-evolving threat landscape. Don't think of this as sinking money into a black hole; think of it as protecting the tangible and intangible assets that make your business thrive now and for years.

Answers To Key Questions

Question 1: How do we calculate the return on investment (ROI) of our cyber initiatives?

Answer: Calculating a traditional ROI for cyber is tricky. After all, you're investing in preventing something that might never happen. However, you can still get a good picture of the potential value.

Here's the approach: instead of pinpointing an exact percentage, focus on estimating the impact. What could a cyber attack potentially cost your business between remediation, lost revenue, and damaged reputation? Compare that potential cost to the cost of implementing your security measures. This gives you a cost-benefit analysis, highlighting how much your investment could save you.

Additionally, threat modeling is crucial. Identify the attacks you're most vulnerable to and what kind of financial hit they'd deliver. Then, prioritize your security spending on protecting against those high-risk threats, maximizing your chances of getting the best return.

Finally, the RoSI (Return on Security Investment) model focuses on avoided losses. While it involves estimation, it's a great way to showcase cyber's value proposition: "We invested X amount in this measure, and we believe it prevented this attack, which typically costs Y."

Of course, ROI is just one piece of the puzzle. Cyber investments also give you something you can't put a price tag on: stronger brand reputation, increased customer trust, and long-term operational peace of mind.

Question 2: What are the most cost-effective cyber measures we can implement?

Answer: Building a solid cyber foundation does not necessarily require a substantial financial investment. A key strategy involves empowering employees, often the first line of defense against cyber threats. Regular security awareness training can help employees identify phishing emails, avoid social engineering traps, and create strong passwords. Such training is relatively inexpensive yet can go a long way in mitigating the risk of security breaches.

In addition to training, utilizing open-source security tools presents a cost-effective solution for enhancing defenses. These tools, which include firewalls and intrusion detection systems, are available at little or no cost. Although they may require technical expertise to deploy effectively, they offer a robust means of protecting against a wide range of cyber threats.

Another critical measure is the regular patching of software and operating systems. Keeping software up to date is essential for closing security vulnerabilities that hackers could exploit. Automating this process ensures that patches are applied consistently and without delay, fortifying security without necessitating continuous manual intervention.

Implementing multi-factor authentication (MFA) adds an additional layer of security beyond traditional passwords. By requiring a second form of verification, such as a text message code or authentication app, MFA significantly complicates unauthorized access to accounts, even if passwords are compromised.

Finally, network segmentation can protect sensitive information by dividing a larger network into smaller, more manageable sections. This strategy limits the impact of a breach to isolated areas of the network, thus preventing widespread damage.

Question 3: How do we justify the cyber budget to stakeholders focused on immediate profits?

Answer: Justifying the cyber budget to stakeholders prioritizing short-term gains involves framing the conversation around immediate and long-term financial impacts. One effective strategy is to highlight the potential costs of a cyber attack, including immediate fixes, lost business, reputational damage, and possible fines. By presenting research on the average costs of cyber incidents within the industry, stakeholders can see the direct financial risks associated with inadequate security measures.

Beyond immediate costs, it's crucial to emphasize that cyber is an investment in the future health of the business. A significant cyber attack can derail projects and disrupt operations, which could erode profits over time. Conversely, a strong security posture reduces downtime and minimizes the expenses associated with crisis management, supporting sustained profitability.

Illustrating the return on investment (ROI) from previous security initiatives can also be persuasive. For example, demonstrating how past investments in employee training reduced the frequency of phishing attacks provides tangible evidence that proactive spending on cyber can yield significant savings by preventing costly breaches.

Moreover, cyber enhances a company's reputation for reliability and trustworthiness, which is increasingly important to customers in today's digital landscape. A secure company not only retains existing customers but also attracts new ones, potentially opening up new markets. Thus, robust cyber can be a competitive advantage, contributing to long-term profitability.

When discussing cyber with stakeholders, tailor the message to align with their interests. For executives, cyber is linked to risk management and shareholder value. For sales and marketing teams, focus on how security underpins customer trust and competitive differentiation.

Ultimately, the goal is to present cyber not just as a necessary cost to prevent disaster but as a strategic investment that enables the company to achieve its profit objectives securely and sustainably.

Question 4: What are the long-term financial risks of underinvesting in cyber?

Answer: Think of your company as a fortress. Underinvesting in cyber is like leaving the gates open and the treasury unguarded. At first, nothing may happen. But every day, the risk grows. Hackers are like an invading army, constantly probing for weaknesses. Perhaps they steal a bit of gold at first - enough to hurt but not cripple you. But their tactics get bolder, and soon enough, they're holding your operations hostage, demanding a ransom that could drain your resources.

Even if you fight them off, the damage is done. Word gets out that your fortress isn't so secure. Customers flee to rivals with stronger walls. Regulators descend, levying heavy fines. And what about those ambitious expansion plans? They're on hold as funds for growth are diverted to patching holes and rebuilding defenses.

This isn't some hypothetical scenario. Every day, businesses fall victim to the ever-evolving cyber threat landscape. The difference between those who survive and those who crumble comes from preparation. Cyber isn't a luxury or an afterthought—it's the foundation upon which your long-term financial health and future success rest.

Question 5: How do we assess the value of cyber investments in terms of brand protection?

Answer: Your brand reputation is intrinsically tied to how securely and responsibly you handle customer data. A significant data breach doesn't just compromise systems - it shatters the trust that forms the foundation of business relationships. Customers who experience the violation of having their personal or financial information exposed will naturally question whether the company values their business. This erosion of trust directly translates to a loss of business, as they take their loyalty (and their dollars) elsewhere, potentially for good.

But the damage doesn't stop at immediate customer churn. A breach can leave a lasting scar on a company's reputation, making it difficult to attract new customers. News of the breach lives on in search results, and the company becomes associated with security lapses rather than the products or services it offers. This negatively impacts growth and can lead to potential partners being reluctant to collaborate. Even financial negotiations can be affected, as lenders or insurers may view the company as a higher risk.

Let's not forget the significant hard costs associated with a breach. Beyond the technical expense of remediation and lost revenue while systems are down, which cuts directly into profits, there's also the threat of regulatory fines and lawsuits - costly consequences companies may have to bear for years after the initial attack.

Conversely, companies known for strong cyber reap the rewards of a positive reputation. In an age of constant hacking threats, consumers increasingly choose to do business with companies they believe prioritize protecting their data. This fosters customer loyalty and becomes a point of competitive differentiation, allowing a secure company to stand out in a crowded market. While putting a precise dollar figure on brand value is impossible, strong cyber undoubtedly contributes to a healthier bottom line through enhanced reputation, increased customer trust, and a reduced likelihood of damaging and costly breaches.

Question 6: What financial metrics can we use to track the effectiveness of our cyber spending?

Answer: Measuring the return on investment (ROI) in cyber can feel like quantifying the value of smoke alarms. While their worth becomes undeniably clear when a fire breaks out, how do you measure their effectiveness in preventing one? Fortunately, we can track several financial metrics to demonstrate the value we're getting from our cyber investments.

The first metric to consider is the frequency and severity of security incidents. If our security posture is improving, we should see a decrease in the number and impact of these events over time. This indicates that our investments in tools, training, and security processes have a tangible effect. Instead of constantly reacting to significant breaches, we're preventing them from happening in the first place. Beware of vanity metrics. A common one is, "We stopped 24,000 attacks on our system." While eye-catching (and may tell you that you have something people want), the objective metric should be how many attacks were successful, what the impact was, and what we have done to improve.

We can also look inward at the cost of remediating those security incidents that do occur. Are we catching them earlier, leading to less downtime and lower restoration expenses? Are we identifying and containing threats before they can spread throughout the network, minimizing the need for costly data recovery efforts? Tracking these remediation costs over time can reveal a positive trend, demonstrating that our investments lead to more efficient incident response.

Looking beyond our own company, industry performance data plays a vital role. Extensive research has been conducted to determine the average cost of a significant data breach across various sectors. While these figures are concerning, they can be a powerful tool. Using them as a benchmark, we can estimate the potential financial impact of a large-scale breach on our company. We can then demonstrate how our cyber investments are lowering this risk exposure year after year. Think of it as the economic equivalent of a fire escape on a high-rise building - it might never be used, but its presence significantly reduces the potential cost of disaster.

It's important to remember that financial metrics only tell part of the story. Cyber investments also contribute to a less quantifiable benefit - a reduced risk profile. While it's challenging to put a dollar figure on "peace of mind," we can track metrics like employee productivity losses or the time spent managing the fallout from a breach. By demonstrating how proactive investments reduce these disruptions, we can paint a clearer picture of the overall return on investment in cyber.

In conclusion, measuring the effectiveness of cyber spending goes beyond simply tracking the cost of security tools. By looking at a combination of metrics—frequency of incidents, remediation costs, breach cost estimates, and even indirect impacts—we can build a compelling case for our cyber investments. This data-driven approach demonstrates the financial value of proactive security measures, justifying continued investment in protecting our company's critical assets.

Question 7: How do we communicate the importance of cyber investments to shareholders?

Answer: Financial considerations are paramount when

communicating with shareholders. They are keenly aware that success depends on maximizing returns while carefully managing risks. Cyber discussions need to be framed through that same financial lens.

Let's start by highlighting the reality of today's business landscape: cyber crime is a massive global industry. No company is immune to hacking attempts, whether large or seemingly unimportant. Ignoring this reality isn't an option, as shareholders expect prudent risk management as part of their investment.

It's crucial to translate these threats into tangible financial consequences. Go beyond vague warnings and outline the genuine costs of a significant breach: expenses related to system restoration, lost revenue while recovering from an outage, potential regulatory fines, and even years-long lawsuits. However, the most significant cost is the erosion of customer trust long after systems are back online, hampering growth and competitive advantage.

To drive the message home, illustrate these consequences with relevant and recent examples of cyber attacks. Highlight breaches at companies in our industry or similarly sized companies. This paints a vivid picture for shareholders that this threat isn't theoretical but a clear and present danger that must be proactively addressed.

But communication can't be solely about the risks. Shareholders need to see that we have a plan. Clearly outline our cyber strategy, detailing our investments in defensive tools, employee training, and incident response protocols. This demonstrates that we aren't simply waiting for an attack to happen but are actively taking steps to reduce the likelihood of a successful breach and minimize the damage should one occur.

Finally, frame cyber spending within the broader context of responsible risk management. Cyber is an essential business cost today, just as we invest in legal compliance or insurance for unforeseen risks. By presenting cyber investments this way, we demonstrate to shareholders that the management team and the Board of Directors take security seriously. This builds confidence that cyber is being treated as a core business concern and prioritized appropriately, protecting the longevity and, ultimately, the profitability of the company and, by extension, the shareholders' investment.

Question 8: How can we integrate cyber spending into financial planning?

Answer: It's time to shift how we think about cyber spending. Instead of treating it as an emergency expense dealt with only after a crisis, we need to integrate it into our regular financial planning. Cyber requires a consistent and predictable budget allocation, just as we allocate funds for essential operational costs like rent or electricity.

This budgeting needs to be proactive rather than reactive. Instead of a lump sum thrown at the latest headline-grabbing vulnerability, we must plan for continuous improvements. Schedule regular updates to our security tools, invest in third-party vulnerability assessments, and provide ongoing staff training to keep our defenses up to date. This incremental approach reduces our risk profile and avoids a panicked scramble for funds when a new attack vector emerges.

This proactive approach directly impacts reducing unexpected expenses. We lower the likelihood of a significant breach by investing in preventative measures like better tools, training, and improved processes. This means we're less likely to endure the high costs of system restoration, lost revenue during downtime, and all the time-consuming fallout of a crisis.

A dedicated "rainy day fund" expressly set aside for incident response is also essential. Even the most well-prepared companies can still be targeted. Having resources earmarked for experts, forensic tools, and potential communication expenses, we can respond quickly without diverting funds from other critical business functions during an emergency.

Crucially, this spending needs to be aligned with our risk

appetite. A thorough analysis of our business—which systems are mission-critical, what data needs utmost protection, and what regulatory standards apply—guides where we focus investments. This targeted approach maximizes our return on cyber spending, ensuring resources are going where they have the greatest potential to reduce risk.

Finally, while the upfront costs of cyber are clear, it's important to frame it as an investment, not just an expense. Strong security reduces our long-term financial risk exposure to disruptive and costly breaches. It can also be a competitive advantage in today's world, attracting clients and partners who demand strong data protection practices. We weave cyber budgeting into our overall financial planning process to ensure a secure and resilient company with a strong economic future.

Question 9: How does our cyber spending align with our risk appetite and profile?

Answer: There's no magic formula for cyber spending - a "one-size-fits-all" approach exposes critical gaps. An effective strategy hinges on understanding our unique risk profile and tailoring our investments accordingly. Every company operates within a specific context, with vulnerabilities based on factors like industry regulations, the type of data we handle, and our overall size and structure. For all organizations, large and small, all aspects of the business should be using a "secure-by-design" approach to ensure all core cyber measures are "baked in" from the start. Retrofitting security measures is always costly and sub-optimal.

The first step is to gain a clear picture of our most critical assets. This involves identifying the systems and data fundamental to our daily operations. What information, if compromised, would cause the most significant disruption or financial loss? Are we dealing with sensitive customer data, intellectual property, or trade secrets? Understanding the value of these assets allows us to prioritize their protection.

Next, we need to assess the potential impact of a breach. This goes beyond simply financial considerations. While lost revenue during downtime is a significant concern, we must also factor in potential reputational damage and the operational challenges of recovering from a cyber attack. A data breach can erode customer trust, making it harder to attract new business. It can also disrupt vital business processes, leading to delays and lost productivity. By considering the full potential impact of a breach, we can make informed decisions about where to invest our cyber resources.

A clear understanding of our assets and the potential threats allows us to define our risk appetite. This means determining how much inherent risk we're willing to accept, as achieving absolute cyber is unrealistic. Due to the nature of their data or industry regulations, some companies may have a very low tolerance for risk, requiring significant security investments. Others may be comfortable with a slightly higher level of risk, allowing for a more balanced approach.

Once we understand our risk profile and appetite, we can strategically allocate our cyber spending. We should prioritize the most critical assets and the highest-impact threats. There's no point in investing heavily in securing a rarely used system if the financial data that fuels our business remains vulnerable. Focusing resources on the areas of greatest potential loss ensures we get the most out of our cyber investments.

Finally, it's important to remember that cyber isn't an isolated concern. It should be considered an essential tool for protecting the company's overall success. By aligning our cyber strategy with our broader business objectives, we ensure that every department works together to create a secure environment that fosters innovation, protects our reputation, and safeguards our revenue streams. This is especially true for an organization's ecosystem - having a shared understanding of strategy, risk, and cyberinvestment with partners and suppliers is critical to any organization's success.

Further Reading

1. Gordon, L. A., & Loeb, M. P. (2006). Managing cyber resources: A cost-benefit analysis. McGraw-Hill.

2. Srinidhi, B., Yan, J., & Tayi, G. K. (2015). Allocation of resources to cyber-security: The effect of misalignment of interest between managers and investors. Decision Support Systems, 75, 49-62. https://doi.org/10.1016/j.dss.2015.04.011

3. Pai, S., Hui, K. L., & Yeo, S. F. (2022). Valuing Cyber Investments through Real Options Analysis: A Systematic Review. Information & Management, 59(5), 103606. https://doi.org/10.1016/j.im.2021.103606

4. Huang, C. D., Hu, Q., & Behara, R. S. (2008). An economic analysis of the optimal information security investment in the case of a risk-averse firm. International Journal of Production Economics, 114(2), 793-804. https://doi.org/10.1016/j.ijpe.2008.04.002

5. Bose, R., & Luo, X. (2014). Investigating security investment impact on firm performance. International Journal of Accounting & Information Management, 22(3), 194-208. https://doi.org/10.1108/IJAIM-11-2013-0066

Chapter 7

Cultivating Cyber Guardians: Building a Human Firewall

Today, when cyber threats constantly evolve, technology alone can't guarantee complete protection. The human element is a critical component of any robust cyber strategy. Employees play a vital role in recognizing and mitigating these threats. This chapter explores the concept of a "human firewall" and the importance of actively empowering employees to safeguard your organization's data and systems.

Empowering Employees: The First Line of Defense

Many cyber attacks exploit human error or use social engineering tactics. A cunningly crafted email, a malicious attachment, or a persuasive social media scam can trick even the most vigilant employees into compromising sensitive information or granting unauthorized access. However, by empowering employees with knowledge and awareness, you can establish a strong human firewall as the first line of defense against cyber threats.

It's crucial to remember that cyber threats can also originate from within the organization. Disgruntled employees, accidental data breaches, or a simple lack of awareness can all contribute to security vulnerabilities. To be truly comprehensive, an effective human firewall strategy must address external and internal threats.

There are numerous benefits to an empowered workforce. Educated employees are less likely to fall victim to phishing scams and social engineering tactics. They develop a critical eye, scrutinizing emails, attachments, and requests for information to avoid compromising sensitive data. Empowered employees who understand the signs of suspicious activity are more likely to identify and report potential cyber threats promptly. Early detection and reporting are critical for minimizing the impact of a cyber attack.

Furthermore, fostering a culture of shared responsibility through employee empowerment improves overall security posture. When employees feel valued and trusted to contribute to cyber, everyone becomes accountable for protecting sensitive information and maintaining a secure work environment. This not only strengthens security but also enhances overall productivity. By understanding cyber threats and practicing safe security habits, employees can avoid common pitfalls that lead to wasted time and disruptions, such as falling victim to phishing scams or accidentally downloading malware.

Designing a Security-Aware Culture

Let's be honest: most security training feels like a chore. To shift that perception, we need to make it engaging and relevant. Regular sessions are vital, but they should be tailored to different job functions - what the finance team needs to know is different from what the marketing team needs to know. Mixing things up with videos, quizzes, and even role-playing scenarios keeps things fresh and combats boredom. Organizations should consider human-centric incident management exercises to reinforce individual learning.

Think of phishing simulations as your practice fire drills. They get the adrenaline going, reveal weak spots under pressure, and help employees develop the instincts to spot a scam a mile away. But follow-up is vital - don't just reveal the fake email; explain why it looked suspicious so they can learn for next time.

Another strategy is finding your security ambassadors - those folks in each department who are already cyber savvy or passionate about protecting the company. Empower them to spread the word, champion initiatives, and answer their colleagues' questions. This peer-to-peer influence is more impactful than any IT department memo.

Finally, keep security top-of-mind all year round. Weave reminders into newsletters and company updates and maybe even have eye-catching posters with security tips. And publicly celebrate those security wins when someone thwarts a phishing attempt or reports a suspicious email. Make a big deal of it. This shows that security vigilance is valued and contributes to the company's success, not just a list of rules to follow. All organizations need a balance here between "carrots and sticks."

Responding to Human Error: Prevention and Mitigation

Even with the best preparation, mistakes happen. The aim is to minimize the damage they cause and turn those mistakes into learning opportunities.

Let's talk about those "just in time" reminders. Think of them like those pop-ups asking, "Are you sure?" when you're about to make a risky online purchase but applied to cyber. A quick question: when someone's about to download a strange file, what can be the difference between a crisis averted and a full-blown breach?

Of course, we can't rely on employees alone. That's where multi-factor authentication (MFA) comes in. Think of it as an extra security guard at the gate. Even if a password is compromised, MFA adds a crucial extra step that often stops attackers.

Then comes the sometimes uncomfortable part: what happens when a breach is suspected? Everyone needs to know the drill - who to report to and what steps to take immediately. A clear incident response plan prevents panic and helps the team contain the damage quickly.

Crucially, we need an environment where reporting mistakes is encouraged, not feared. Blaming individuals leads to hiding problems, which is far more dangerous in the long run. Focus on reporting quickly, analyzing why the issue happened, and determining how to prevent it next time. This approach is what makes us more resilient in the long term.

Answers To Key Questions

Question 1: How do we empower employees to become proactive defenders against cyber threats?

Answer: Think of your employees as your company's first line of defense. Too often, they see cyber as a list of rules or obstacles to getting their work done. Our job is to change that perception, transforming them from passive rule-followers into vigilant protectors.

It starts with knowledge. Regular training shouldn't feel like a lecture—instead, it should make employees feel like they're getting the inside scoop on how cyber criminals operate, the tricks they use, and how to spot them a mile away. Simulations are vital, too—like unexpected practice drills, they keep employees on their toes and reveal where more training is needed. And let's make learning fun! A little gamification can turn security lessons into a competition.

But knowledge only gets you so far. We need to equip them with user-friendly tools. If security software is clunky or confusing, employees will find shortcuts, and that's how cracks form. , And, make getting help just a click away - sometimes, a tiny pop-up reminder about a suspicious link is all it takes to prevent a disaster.

Most importantly, create a culture where employees feel empowered. Encourage questions, even if they seem simple. Make it clear that reporting something suspicious is always the right call, even if it turns out to be nothing. And when someone goes the extra mile to protect the company? Publicly celebrate it! This shows security isn't a burden but a way to contribute to the company's success.

The aim is to create a shift - from seeing security as someone else's problem to feeling that personal sense of responsibility. When your employees are armed with knowledge, understand the "why" behind security measures, and think like key players in protecting the company, that's when you've built a compelling defense.

Question 2: What are the most effective methods to foster a security-aware culture within our company?

Answer: Building a security-conscious company isn't about a single training session or a scary memo. It's about embedding security into the company's DNA, making it as natural as checking your work twice or hitting deadlines. To achieve that, we need a constant, multi-pronged approach.

First, security needs to be heard and seen everywhere. Weave reminders into newsletters, internal messaging, and even during team meetings. Make cyber a shared responsibility, not just (wrongly) an IT department concern.

And this can't just be talk - leaders need to champion security visibly. Strong passwords and careful communication shouldn't be secrets but examples from the top down. When employees see leadership taking this seriously, it has a ripple effect.

Let's make learning engaging, not a chore. Ditch the boring lectures and try interactive videos, quizzes, and even friendly competition. And find your champions - the naturally security-savvy folks in every department. Empowering them to spread the word to their peers carries far more weight than any IT team could.

The goal is for cyber to become second nature. We want employees to pause before clicking a strange link, not because they fear punishment but because they recognize the signs of a threat and take pride in stopping it. That's real culture change and the foundation of a genuinely resilient company.

Lastly, you must build a "cyber contract" with your workforce. One tried and tested way is for the organization to guide employees securely using social media by giving them up-to-date information on settings for popular social media platforms like Facebook. Secondly, they also provide helpful tips for their children and older relatives who are more likely to be victims of "Vishing" than any other societal demographic. Employees will see that the organization is trying to help them, and the organization can then remind them not to divulge company business on social media feeds. All this contributes immensely to building a positive cyber secure culture.

Question 3: How do we address and mitigate human error regarding cyber?

Answer: Even the most security-conscious employee will make the occasional slip-up. The key isn't to prevent every mistake but to limit the damage they cause and turn them into learning experiences.

Think of it like those pop-up reminders when you're about to make a risky online purchase - but applied to cyber. When downloading a strange attachment, a quick "Are you sure?" could distinguish between a crisis averted and a full-blown breach.

Of course, you can't rely on employees alone. Even if someone's password is compromised, things like multi-factor authentication can still stop an attacker in their tracks. These systems work like safety nets, giving us a margin for error.

Then comes the sometimes uncomfortable part: analyzing mistakes. This isn't about punishment; it's about finding the weak points. Maybe a phishing email was cleverly disguised, revealing a gap in training. Or an incident that shows the need for more transparent reporting procedures. Each mistake is a chance to make the company more resilient.

Crucially, you need a culture where employees feel safe reporting those mistakes. Fear of getting in trouble leads to hiding problems, which is far more dangerous. By encouraging open communication and focusing on solutions, not blame, you get the information needed to act quickly and improve your defenses.

The goal is to move from a mindset of fearing errors to one of outsmarting them. By combining smart reminders, layered security, and a focus on continuous improvement, you can make human error a far less dangerous threat to your company's security.

Question 4: What training initiatives can we implement to strengthen our human firewall?

Answer: Let's be honest: Most security training feels like eating your vegetables - necessary but not exciting. Our challenge is transforming training from a chore into something empowering for our employees.

Start with relevance. Not everyone needs the same level of technical detail. Train the finance team to spot fraudulent invoices while sales reps learn to double-check links before clicking. This tailored approach means every minute feels valuable and well-spent.

Let's embrace bite-sized learning. Long lectures lead to glazed-over eyes. Think short, impactful videos, interactive quizzes, and a quick mobile game that teaches phishing red flags. This keeps things fresh and better suits modern attention spans.

Practice makes perfect. Simulations are a must - like fire drills, they reveal weak points under pressure. But let's add in role-playing, too! Have someone act out a social engineering scam and see who can spot the manipulation. It's more memorable than any slideshow.

The goal isn't just remembering rules but applying them in

the real world. Scenario-based training drops employees into a situation and makes them decide how to act. Do they open that strange email? Do they share sensitive data? This kind of training helps them build the instincts to make good choices.

Finally, keep security top-of-mind all year round with engaging campaigns - posters, contests, maybe even a "weirdest phishing attempt of the month" leaderboard to add some humor. It's about reminding everyone they play a vital role in protecting the company.

Question 5: How can we measure the effectiveness of our cyber awareness programs?

Answer: Think of training as building a fortress and metrics as your watchtowers. You can't just assume the walls are strong - you need constant feedback to know if they're doing their job.

Here's where you start: Are people even showing up for the fight? Tracking who completes training gives us a basic idea of engagement. But of course, showing up doesn't mean they learned anything. That's where simulations come in. Lower click rates on fake phishing attempts and more reported scams are signs our training is having a real-world impact.

Next, do they understand the "why" behind security? Pre- and post-training quizzes reveal if the lessons truly stuck. Plus, if incident reports increase after training, that's a good sign (as long as they're the right kind of reports, of course!) It means employees are more alert.

But numbers only tell part of the story. You need to talk to your "troops" - surveys and feedback sessions let us know if training feels relevant and helpful or confusing and pointless. And don't forget about the big picture: Are people less likely to click risky links out of habit, and is "think before you click" becoming the office motto? These culture shifts are more complex to quantify but vital to success.

The key is designing your awareness program with measurement in mind. By choosing the right mix of metrics, you gain insights that train employees and build a genuinely unbreakable human firewall.

Question 6: How can we create a sense of ownership and responsibility for cyber among all employees?

Answer: Too often, employees see cyber as someone else's problem - the IT department, maybe leadership. You must aim to change that perception and make everyone realize they play a vital role in protecting the company.

It starts with awareness of the stakes. Don't just throw out scary stats - explain how a breach could impact their jobs, disrupt projects, and even damage the company's reputation with customers. When it feels personal, people pay closer attention.

Connect it to their daily work. Don't just list rules; help them see how clicking a bad link or leaving sensitive data out could have real consequences. Specific examples make this feel real, not abstract.

Then, empower them! Complex security software and confusing policies create apathy and workarounds. Give employees the tools and knowledge to do the right thing easily. Plus, celebrate the wins - publicly recognizing someone who thwarted a phishing attempt shows that good security practices are valued and noticed.

Finally, foster a sense of teamwork. Encourage questions! Make it clear that reporting something suspicious is always the right call, even if it turns out to be nothing. Security champions in each department can spread the word more relatably than any IT memo ever could.

The goal is to shift from seeing security as a list of chores to feeling a personal sense of responsibility for the company's well-being when your employees understand the "why" behind security measures and feel like key players in the company's digital defense, you've built a potent force.

Question 7: How can we integrate cyber awareness into the onboarding process for new hires?

Answer: Think of the new-hire onboarding process as the first day of school at a superhero academy. Sure, they get their costume and learn to fly, but they also learn the rules that keep everyone safe. Cyber needs to be woven in from the start.

A dedicated training session is essential, but make it about understanding rather than memorizing. Ditch the boring slideshow and focus on the "why." Why do strong passwords matter? Why is clicking strange links dangerous? Use real examples to bring the risks home, especially if they relate to your industry.

Let's make it hands-on. Simple scenarios where the new hire has to decide if something is a security risk gets them thinking critically. It's more memorable than any lecture. Plus, having them clearly acknowledge your security policies - not just signing, but explaining what they mean in plain terms - shows that this is serious business, not red tape. Research shows that, especially if the environment is complex, a follow-up session within three months of starting a new role helps cement learning, as many new starts don't absorb too much during the induction process.

The goal is to build a security mindset from day one. New employees should understand that protecting the company isn't just an extra task; it's part of being a good team member. By laying this foundation early, we make security feel like second nature, preventing bad habits from ever forming.

Question 8: What role does leadership play in responding to incidents caused by human error?

Answer: How leadership reacts to a security incident caused by human error can shape how the company views these situations. The wrong response breeds fear and cover-ups; the right one creates an opportunity for improvement.

It starts with empathy. Remember, even the most careful employee can slip up. Jumping to blame shuts down communication, dooming us to repeat the same mistakes. Leaders should focus on asking "why" this happened, not "who" to punish.

Transparency is key. Rumors spread fast after an incident. Leaders who explain what went wrong and, more importantly, how it's being fixed rebuild trust and show that security is a priority.

And crucially, leadership needs to walk the walk. If employees see leaders taking shortcuts or disregarding policies, the message is clear: it's unimportant. Leaders should be role models for good cyber practices, demonstrating commitment and accountability.

The goal is to transform mistakes into catalysts for improvement. After an incident, the question shouldn't be, "Who messed up?" but "How do we make sure this doesn't happen again?" With the proper leadership response, even a human error can strengthen the company's defenses.

Question 9: How do we maintain and update our cyber training to keep pace with emerging threats?

Answer: Think of your cyber training like a superhero's arsenal - it can't stay the same if the villains constantly acquire new weapons. Staying ahead of the bad guys means being agile and adaptable in how you train your employees.

First, you need constant intel. The security landscape is dynamic, so our training must also be dynamic. You need to keep tabs on the latest types of attacks and the tricks hackers are using, and that knowledge needs to be woven into training ASAP. Industry updates are your superpower here!

Make training modular. Think of it like switching out attachments on a toolbelt. You can quickly swap in updated training if a new phishing technique emerges. There's no need to wait for a full-blown course redesign every time.

Let's keep things interesting. Bite-sized learning, even a little friendly competition - these techniques go a long way in combating training fatigue. Regular campaigns with posters, quizzes, and updates remind people that this isn't a once-a-year chore but an ongoing battle.

The goal is to create training that feels as responsive and dynamic as the cyber landscape. When employees see that their knowledge is always up to date, they'll be more confident and engaged in staying one step ahead of the bad guys.

Cultivating a human firewall is an ongoing process that requires commitment, creativity, and constant adaptation. By empowering employees with knowledge, fostering a security-aware culture, and turning mistakes into learning opportunities, you can transform your workforce from potential weak points into a formidable line of defense.

Remember, cyber isn't just the IT department's job. It's a shared responsibility that touches every corner of the company. When every employee, from the C-suite to the front lines, understands their role and feels invested in protecting the company, we create a resilient organization.

Question 10. How can organizations extend their culture of security beyond their full-time, in-office staff?

Answer: Organizations should take a proactive, inclusive approach that considers remote workers' and third-party partners' unique risks and needs.

Start by clearly communicating your security policies and expectations to all stakeholders, regardless of their location or affiliation. This includes providing regular training and awareness programs tailored to the specific roles and responsibilities of remote employees, contractors, and suppliers.

Next, technical controls like virtual private networks (VPNs), multi-factor authentication (MFA), and data loss prevention (DLP) tools should be implemented to secure remote access to company systems and data. Establish clear procedures for securely onboarding and offboarding remote workers and third-party users, including provisioning and revoking access privileges.

Follow up with regular assessments of the security posture of your supply chain partners, including their adherence to your policies and any regulatory requirements. This may involve questionnaires, audits, or contractual obligations.

Foster open lines of communication and provide channels for remote workers and partners to report security concerns or incidents.

Finally, lead by example. Ensure your remote workforce, and executives are held to the same high-security hygiene and behavior standards.

Further Reading

1. Mitnick, K. D., & Simon, W. L. (2002). The art of deception: Controlling the human element of security. Wiley.

2. Hadnagy, C. (2010). Social engineering: The art of human hacking. Wiley.

3. Cialdini, R. B. (2021). Influence: The psychology of persuasion. Harper Business.

4. Caputo, D. D., Pfleeger, S. L., Freeman, J. D., & Johnson, M. E. (2014). Going spear phishing: Exploring embedded training and awareness. IEEE Security & Privacy, 12(1), 28-38. https://doi.org/10.1109/MSP.2013.106

5. Kumaraguru, P., Sheng, S., Acquisti, A., Cranor, L. F., & Hong, J. (2010). Teaching Johnny not to fall for phish. ACM Transactions on Internet Technology (TOIT), 10(2), 1-31. https://doi.org/10.1145/1754393.1754396

Chapter 8

Securing The Supply Chain Ecosystem

With the current hyper-connectivity of devices, sensors, and networks, your company doesn't exist in a vacuum. The businesses you partner with - your suppliers, vendors, and third-party services - are woven into the fabric of your operations. This brings fantastic benefits but also means their security weaknesses become yours. A breach at a seemingly unimportant supplier could give attackers a back door into your systems. Over the last three years, around 80% of the major breaches in all sectors have been perpetrated through the supply chain. That's why supply chain cyber is now essential.

Understanding Your Supply Chain Vulnerabilities

The first step to building a secure supply chain is understanding where the potential cracks are. Start by mapping out your entire network. This isn't just a list of companies you work with - think of it as a blueprint. What data do they have access to? What systems, or even physical locations, do they interact with? Once you visualize this flow of information, you start seeing the entry points for attackers.

Now, it's time for critical self-examination. Conduct security assessments on your systems (don't assume your house is in order!) and extend these to your key suppliers. Look for common security weak points - outdated software, bad password practices, or any gaps a clever hacker could exploit.

But remember, technology isn't the whole picture. Disgruntled employees with access to sensitive data or vendors easily targeted with social engineering tricks are vulnerabilities, too. And remember that suppliers have their own suppliers! Your comprehensive risk analysis needs to consider this entire chain of trust.

Fostering a Culture of Cyber Resilience Across the Ecosystem

Building proper security across your supply chain means going beyond tech fixes. Think of it like a neighborhood watch - you want everyone invested in keeping things safe. This starts with clear, legally binding contracts that set cyber expectations. Spell out exactly how suppliers should handle your data, their responsibility in case of a breach, and what security standards they must meet.

However, contracts alone aren't enough. You need open communication with your partners about cyber threats. Share information and best practices and create a sense that you're all facing these threats together. Think about collaborations with critical suppliers around security - maybe sharing threat intelligence data or even having joint security assessments.

Don't forget the power of training! Extending your security awareness programs to include vendors ups everyone's game. When the receptionist at your logistics partner knows how to spot a phishing email, that protects your data, too.

Proactive and Reactive Measures to Secure the Supply Chain

So, what are the practical steps you and your partners can take? First, let's look at the whole value chain of the business. In the next section, we will deal specifically with IT outsourcing. It's a mix of preventing attacks and being prepared if the worst happens:

- *Proactive:* This starts with procurement. Good cyber practices must be implemented at all stages of procurement, including the final contract. We and the ecosystem partners must have recognized information exchange and data security management governance structures. In terms of technology, encourage secure software development practices across your whole chain. This means your developers and ensuring your suppliers have secure coding, testing, and update procedures, too. Multi-factor authentication (MFA) is another essential - that extra layer of login security makes it harder for attackers to break in, even with a stolen password. Finally, strong protocols and policies on exchanging and managing business data must be enforced. For instance, in data retention, if a supplier doesn't need sensitive information to do their job, they shouldn't have it - this reduces the potential fallout if they are breached.

- *Reactive:* Having a plan isn't pessimistic; it's realistic. Your incident response plan needs to cover what happens if there's a breach anywhere in the supply chain. Who needs to be notified, what steps are taken to solve the problem, and how do you quickly get systems back online? This should be planned and drilled in advance, just like a fire alarm plan! Be sure to have clear communication protocols about breaches - no one wants to discover from the news that their supplier was hacked.

- *Continuous Improvement:* As threats evolve, so must your defenses. Regularly review and update your security measures to account for the supply chain. Track how you're doing - are specific successful attacks happening less often? This tells you which efforts are working. Share security metrics with your vendors and partners - transparency builds trust and motivates everyone to strive higher.

The Challenge of Secure Outsourcing

As organizations increasingly outsource critical functions to cloud providers, it is crucial to ensure these partners adhere to robust security standards. Start by thoroughly vetting potential cloud providers, looking for those with solid track records, relevant certifications (e.g., ISO 27001, SOC 2), and a transparent approach to security.

When drafting service level agreements (SLAs), include specific security requirements, metrics, and provisions for regular audits and assessments. Maintain open lines of communication with your cloud providers to stay informed about their security practices, incident response plans, and any changes that could impact your data or applications.

Implement strong access controls and monitoring for your cloud environments, and consider strategies like encryption and tokenization to protect sensitive data even if the underlying infrastructure is compromised.

Review and test your cloud security posture regularly, and consider engaging third-party experts to conduct assessments or penetration tests. By taking a proactive, layered approach to cloud security oversight, organizations can reap the benefits of cloud computing while minimizing risks.

The impact of AI and IoT on Supply chain considerations

Automation and artificial intelligence (AI) can be powerful tools for scaling and enhancing supply chain security efforts. With the vast amounts of data generated across complex supplier networks, manual analysis and monitoring can quickly become overwhelming.

AI-powered solutions can continuously monitor supplier risk data from various sources (e.g., financial reports, news feeds, dark web forums) and use machine learning algorithms to identify patterns or anomalies that may indicate potential issues. This enables organizations to proactively detect and respond to emerging supplier risks that might otherwise go unnoticed.

Automation can also streamline and standardize key supply chain security processes, such as vendor onboarding and off-boarding, risk assessments, and compliance audits. Organizations can free up their security teams to focus on more strategic initiatives and high-value investigations by automating repetitive, time-consuming tasks.

However, it's important to remember that AI and automation are not silver bullets. These technologies should augment, not replace, human expertise and decision-making. Organizations must ensure that their AI models are trained on diverse, unbiased data and regularly tested for accuracy and fairness. There should also be transparent human review and intervention processes in case of false positives or high-stakes decisions.

When implemented thoughtfully, AI and automation can be valuable assets in the ongoing battle to secure increasingly complex and interconnected supply chains.

Securing your supply chain is an investment in your business's future health. By taking ownership of potential vulnerabilities, fostering a sense of shared responsibility with your partners, and having proactive and reactive plans in place, you'll create a more robust, more resilient business ecosystem. Effective procurement is critical.

Answers To Key Questions

Question 1: What strategies are we employing to ensure our supply chain partners adhere to our cyber standards?

Answer: You don't want your strong security to be undone by a weak link in your supply chain. That's why you must take a multifaceted approach to ensuring that your partners are as serious about cyber as you are.

It starts with your procurement strategy and legal groundwork. Your contracts with suppliers have crystal-clear cyber clauses that define the security standards they must meet (think of them as the "rules of the road"). These contracts specify how, why, and where data exchange should occur. Governance is critical here; aligning accountabilities and responsibilities with appropriate authority will give a practical framework across the ecosystem for managing cyber risks. Technology should specify what kind of encryption they should use for sensitive data, multi-factor authentication to protect logins, and the need to immediately report any breach, or even a suspected breach, to us. You should also reserve the right to audit your partners' systems to ensure they meet these standards.

But it's not just about paperwork. Before signing a contract, potential suppliers must complete a detailed security questionnaire. This gives you a good picture of their current security practices and highlights any red flags or areas they may need to improve before working with you.

You should take a collaborative approach, too. You should provide security awareness training to your partners, covering the basics of what threats to look out for and how their actions impact your data security. Finally, you should incentivize good security! Partners who demonstrate commitment to cyber may get priority for new contracts, discounts, or public recognition. This shows that you're serious and makes prioritizing security a win-win for your partners.

You're making security a shared responsibility across your supply network by combining legal agreements, assessments, training, and this "carrot and stick" approach.

Question 2: How do we evaluate the effectiveness of our cyber initiatives across the supply chain?

Answer: Implementing security measures and hoping for the best is not enough. You need a system to constantly measure how well things are working within your company and with your supply chain partners.

Use a mix of proactive and reactive techniques. Regularly scheduled security audits - like a deep-dive checkup - are essential to look for gaps in defenses and ensure that you and your partners follow agreed-upon security practices.

But day-to-day tracking is essential, too. Define key performance indicators (KPIs) to monitor security health. These might include the number of security issues fixed monthly, the percentage of suppliers' staff completing training, or how quickly breaches are spotted and fixed. Tracking these over time shows if any areas are worsening (needing more focus) or if your initiatives are making a positive difference.

Invest in technology that gives you real-time insights. A System Information and Event Management (SIEM) system gathers security data from your network, including your partners, as an early warning system for unusual activity. Finally, regularly review your suppliers' overall security performance - are they reporting incidents quickly? Do they actively participate in your training programs? This comprehensive approach helps you spot potential problems early and constantly refine your strategy for maximum security across the supply chain.

Question 3: What mechanisms have we established to respond rapidly and mitigate supply chain cyber incidents?

Answer: When it comes to cyber attacks, every second counts. Have a detailed plan tailored specifically to breaches across your supply chain. It's unrealistic to think you can prevent every attack, but you can minimize the damage through swift action.

The cornerstone of this is your Incident Response Plan. It's a step-by-step playbook(s) for dealing with a breach, which we cover in more detail and provide a template for in our other book, "Cyber for Executives Simplified". How do you spot an issue in the first place? This might involve a combination of automated alerts and reports from your partners. Once an attack is detected, the plan details how it's contained to prevent spread, how the threat is eradicated, and how you get systems back online quickly. The plan outlines a clear communication chain - who needs to know what, when, to coordinate the response and prevent wasted time.

Have a specialized incident response team, too. These folks aren't just IT - they come from different departments like legal and procurement, ensuring all angles are covered. This team trains together regularly, so everyone knows their role when a breach happens. Cyber leaders need to train to lead; if their first experience of managing a breach is an actual incident, then the chances are they will fail.

Finally, collaboration with your partners is critical. Maintain clear communication channels and emphasize the importance of reporting any suspicious activity immediately. Catching an attack early is often the key to stopping it before it gets serious. You should also plug into industry-wide threat-sharing networks, so that if another company in your sector discovers a new attack method, you get an early warning. Typically this is done by the Security and Information Risk Officer (SIRO) or Chief Information Security Officer (CISO), but you can allocate dedicated executives, such as the Chief Procurement Officer, depending on the type of organization and the cyber knowledge of individuals.

With a comprehensive plan, a well-prepared team, and a collaborative approach across your network, you will have confidence that you can rapidly respond to any cyber attack and minimize the impact on your business and customers.

Question 4: To what extent are we leveraging technology to secure our supply chain from cyber threats?

Answer: Technology is one of your most potent weapons in the fight against cybercrime, and you must use it strategically to protect your entire supply chain. Firstly, automate many routine security tasks. The software handles tasks like scanning systems for vulnerabilities, managing access permissions, and even initial incident response steps. This saves time and ensures that crucial checks don't get overlooked due to human error.

Secondly, place a heavy emphasis on continuous monitoring. Think of this as having security cameras throughout the supply chain network. Special software analyzes patterns in network traffic, looking for anything out of the ordinary that might suggest an attack is building. This early warning system gives you a massive advantage in stopping threats quickly.

Of course, protecting the data itself is a priority. Insist on strong encryption both when data is at rest (being stored) and "in transit" (moving between partners). This means that even if attackers manage to intercept data, it's scrambled and useless to them. Ensure that you have strict data loss prevention (DLP) systems in place. These track how sensitive data moves, and if anything unusual happens - like a large file being sent to a personal email address - it raises an alert.

Finally, secure collaboration tools are essential. When sharing sensitive files with partners, use platforms explicitly designed for security. They provide access controls (so only authorized people can see specific information), strong encryption, and even leave a trail of who accessed what for forensic purposes if needed.

Technology gives you far greater reach and vigilance across a complex supply chain network by using automation, monitoring, data protection, and secure communication.

Question 5: How are we fostering a culture of cyber awareness among our suppliers and partners?

Answer: You know that technology alone isn't enough. To truly secure your supply chain, you need everyone involved to understand the threats and feel invested in protecting themselves - and, by extension, protecting the organization. Here's how you can make that happen:

First and foremost, you need to ensure that our partners have just as effective a governance chain for cyber as you do, with specialist roles trained and working in collaboration with you. Next, provide comprehensive training tailored to your partners. This isn't just a generic security slideshow - it teaches them how their work intersects with cyber, the kinds of attacks they need to watch out for, and how good habits like strong passwords and spotting phishing emails help everyone. Most importantly, emphasize how to report something suspicious and that there's never shame in asking questions.

You should not stop at one-time training. Cyber changes quickly, so use regular webinars and centralized online resources to share new information continually. Suppliers know where to find the latest best practices, threat updates, and reminders about security protocols.

Organize joint workshops with key partners. This isn't you lecturing them - it's about sharing knowledge and fostering collaboration. These workshops let you all share challenges and brainstorm solutions together, which shows your commitment and makes security feel like a team effort, not something imposed from the outside.

Finally, celebrate success! Publicly recognize suppliers who demonstrate a commitment to strong security, which shows that you value it and incentivizes other partners to improve their practices. You may even develop a rating system that lets suppliers benchmark themselves against others, creating healthy competition around security.

The goal is to move beyond seeing cyber as a chore imposed upon your suppliers. You want to create a culture where everyone sees themselves as a line of defense. By providing knowledge, tools, collaboration, and recognition of achievement, strong cyber becomes its reward for your partners.

Question 6: What are our criteria for selecting secure supply chain partners?

Answer: Choosing the right partners is your first line of defense against supply chain attacks. You must carefully vet potential suppliers, prioritizing those demonstrating their cyber commitment. Here's what you must focus on:

First, look for specific recognized standards your potential partners might have achieved to gauge their cyber maturity. Then, check that robust and well-documented security policies underpin these standards and that these are, in turn, board-led and have translated into proactive governance structures. This shows you that they take security seriously and have invested in proactive planning. While certification isn't a guarantee of perfect security, it signals that a supplier is willing to subject themselves to independent audits and is actively working to improve their practices.

Of course, you want to know how these principles translate into action. Before bringing a new partner on board, have them complete a detailed security questionnaire that examines their data handling practices, access controls, incident response, and more. You may even conduct an on-site audit for critical suppliers, getting a firsthand look at how their security works in the real world.

You should also consider a supplier's track record. Have they had any publicly known data breaches in the past? How do others in the industry view them in terms of security? This gives you a sense of their overall commitment to security over time. Finally, assess their disaster recovery plans. Even a supplier with excellent security practices must be able to bounce back from disruptions, or their problems become your problems.

By carefully considering these factors, you build a well-rounded picture of a potential partner's security posture. This allows you to choose suppliers with confidence that share your commitment to protecting sensitive data and align with our security standards.

Question 7: How do we maintain dynamic and responsive cyber practices as new threats emerge?

Answer: The cyber world, with hostile state actors and international organized crime groups, never sleeps, so your defenses can't either! Have a multi-pronged approach designed to stay ahead of the curve. The first step is being informed - subscribe to threat intelligence feeds, participate in industry conferences, and actively network with other security professionals. This gives you insights into the latest attack methods being used so that you can update your defenses before those threats hit your doorstep.

This information isn't just for your IT team. Constantly update your security awareness training to reflect the changing threat landscape. Attackers love using new social engineering tricks, so it's crucial to ensure employees and partners know the latest techniques for spotting phishing red flags and social media attack vectors.

Have a philosophy of continuous assessment. Regularly scheduled security audits for your systems and critical partners act as an "early warning system" for new vulnerabilities. You should also believe in testing your defenses through penetration testing. This involves hiring ethical hackers to try to break in, showing you where to strengthen your defenses before real criminals find those weaknesses.

Technology is also critical to responsive defense. Use various automation tools to streamline vulnerability scanning, patching systems quickly, and even some automated aspects of incident response. This means you can react much faster to emerging threats, minimizing the window of opportunity for attackers. You should also investigate more advanced Security Orchestration and Automation Platforms (SOAR), which can further streamline and speed up your responses, giving you the edge in a fast-evolving environment.

The key is never to become complacent. By embracing this blend of proactive intelligence, continuous assessment, and technology, you ensure that your cyber posture evolves as quickly as the threats you face.

Question 8: How can we enhance our incident response plan to include comprehensive supply chain considerations?

Answer: There must be more than a standard incident response plan when your business network includes numerous partners and suppliers. Here's how to make sure your plan is ready to tackle breaches that extend across your entire supply chain:

First, it all starts with understanding your risk. A detailed supply chain risk assessment is essential. This identifies the most critical suppliers and the potential weak points in their systems that could become our weak points. This information informs your whole response plan, prioritizing where your efforts will have the most impact.

Next comes communication. The plan needs to clearly outline the communication chain during an attack. Who notifies affected suppliers or customers? Who keeps regulatory bodies in the loop? What information needs to be shared at each stage? Having this defined in advance means no time is wasted figuring out who should talk to whom when seconds count.

Crucially, your plan needs to detail how you'll work with suppliers during a breach. What are their responsibilities if they are the source of the attack? What information are they obligated to share with you? What role will they play in recovery efforts?

You must also ensure that the incident response plan fits hand-in-glove with your broader third-party risk management program. These shouldn't be separate documents - they need to use the same definitions and processes, ensuring no confusion if an incident occurs.

And like any plan, it needs testing. You should regularly run tabletop exercises that simulate supply-chain-specific attack scenarios. This lets you see if the plan works in theory, test communication under pressure, and ensure that everyone, including your suppliers, knows their role during a crisis.

Finally, this plan needs to be a living document. Your supply chain changes, threats evolve, and you learn from every exercise. Regular reviews and updates ensure the plan is a reliable tool, ready to guide practical efforts across your entire supply chain ecosystem if an attack happens.

Question 9: How can we better integrate cyber risk management into our overall supply chain risk management framework?

Answer: Historically, supply chain risk management focused on disruptions like natural disasters or financial problems at suppliers. But it's time to expand this view to prioritize cyber as a core part of your risk assessment. Here's how to make that shift:

First, you need a common language for evaluating risk. Develop a standard methodology that your teams use for all assessments, considering traditional supply chain risks and cyber vulnerabilities. This ensures that everyone is speaking the same language and eliminates any blind spots in how we evaluate suppliers.

Next, we need to prioritize based on impact. Some suppliers are more critical to your operation than others, and some handle more sensitive data. Cyber risks need to be assessed in this context. The security practices of the company that supplies your cafeteria are less of a concern than the company that has access to your customer records!

Collaboration is another critical piece of the puzzle. Security, procurement, and supply chain teams must be on the same page. This shared understanding of risks allows for better decision-making and coordinated strategies that address all types of risk. Integrating cyber assessments into your standard supplier onboarding and monitoring process aligns everyone's efforts.

Finally, like any business process, you need to track how you're doing. Develop specific KPIs (key performance indicators) that measure the integration of cyber into the broader risk management framework. Metrics like the number of cyber vulnerabilities discovered in suppliers, their security improvement over time, and your responsiveness to breaches that originate with them are good starting points. Regularly tracking and analyzing this data shows you where your strategies are working and where you might need a new approach.

By adopting a more holistic approach to supply chain risk assessment, fostering collaboration across teams, and committing to data-driven decision-making, you can seamlessly weave cyber into the existing risk management framework. This ensures that all potential threats, including cyber threats, are evaluated and addressed, leading to a more resilient and secure business.

Further Reading

1. Shackelford, S. J., & Craig, A. N. (2014). Beyond the new "digital divide": Analyzing the evolving role of national governments in Internet governance and enhancing cyber. Stanford Journal of International Law, 50(1), 119-184. https://ssrn.com/abstract=2448190

2. Boyens, J., Paulsen, C., Moorthy, R., & Bartol, N. (2015). Supply chain risk management practices for federal information systems and organizations. NIST Special Publication 800-161. https://doi.org/10.6028/NIST.SP.800-161

3. Manners-Bell, J. (2017). Supply chain risk management: Understanding emerging threats to global supply chains (2nd ed.). Kogan Page.

4. Ghadge, A., Weiß, M., Caldwell, N. D., & Wilding, R. (2020). Managing cyber risk in supply chains: A review and research agenda. Supply Chain Management: An International Journal, 25(2), 223-240. https://doi.org/10.1108/SCM-10-2018-0357

5. Yoon, J., Talluri, S., Yildiz, H., & Ho, W. (2018). Models for supplier selection and risk mitigation: A holistic approach. International Journal of Production Research, 56(10), 3636-3661. https://doi.org/10.1080/00207543.2017.1403662

Chapter 9

Proactive Cyber Incident Management

Today, cyber attacks are a constant threat. Organizations of all sizes are vulnerable to data breaches, malware infections, and other security incidents. A proactive cyber incident management (CIM) plan is crucial for minimizing damage, protecting sensitive information, and ensuring business continuity. Let's delve into the essential steps of proactive incident management, focusing on first response, effective communication, and a smooth recovery process.

Mastering the First Response

The initial hours and days following a cyber attack are a race against time. A swift, coordinated first response is the key to minimizing the incident's impact and getting recovery underway. There are two critical components to this:

First, you need to be able to spot an attack early. Security tools like SIEM, IDS/IPS systems, and endpoint security solutions monitor your network constantly, looking for anything unusual that could signal an intrusion. But your best detectors might be your employees - train them to report any strange system behavior or suspicious emails. Many organizations also monitor social media, which is often the first to react and give details of the impact of a successful attack. The faster you realize you have a problem, the less time attackers have to cause damage.

Once you suspect a problem, the second component, speed, is essential. If it's potentially a big problem, activate your Incident Response Team (IRT) - you can always stand them down if things aren't as bad as first thought. Think about containing the threat by immediately isolating affected systems to prevent further spread of the compromise, like firefighters trying to stop a fire from spreading. This could mean disconnecting infected systems from the network, locking compromised user accounts, and doing anything else to stop the attack from doing more damage. Simultaneously, suppose it's a direct threat to your systems. In that case, your IT team must eradicate the threat - removing malware, patching any security holes the attackers used, and getting systems clean again.

But it's not just about the tech - your IRT must be ready to act. This cross-departmental team, including people from IT, legal, PR, and business operations, needs to know their roles well in advance. Regular training exercises ensure they understand their responsibilities and are ready to work together smoothly during an attack.

Also, prepare detailed playbooks for common types of attacks. These step-by-step plans save precious time and ensure nothing vital gets overlooked in the heat of the moment. Crucially, you must keep detailed, up-to-date inventories of your hardware and software and where you store critical data to make these containment and recovery processes far more efficient.

Next, preserve evidence for forensic analysis. This includes creating disk images, capturing memory dumps, and logging all actions taken during the response process. Use this evidence to investigate the scope and origin of the breach thoroughly. Look for indicators of compromise, such as unusual network traffic, suspicious processes, or unauthorized user activity.

Communicating Under Fire

During a cyber incident, how you communicate is just as important as the technical response. Here's what you need to keep in mind:

Start with your organization (Board and employees). After a breach, they're going to be worried. Communicate honestly about what happened, how it might affect them, and most importantly, what you're doing to fix it. Keeping people informed reduces anxiety and builds trust. For most organizations, maintaining a "business-as-usual" approach can be critical for many reasons, and the organization must understand who is doing what.

You'll also need to decide who to inform outside the company---customers, partners, and, where appropriate, regulators. Each group will need tailored communications---customers mostly care if their data is stolen, whereas partners might need more technical information to protect their systems. Having pre-drafted templates for these communications, approved by legal, will save time and ensure everyone gets consistent information. It's also crucial to designate media-trained spokespersons so you have a single, authoritative voice communicating with the outside world.

Transparency is critical, but you can't reveal anything that would let the attackers exploit you further. It's a balancing act! Be open and honest about what you can share, but be mindful of security, especially during the ongoing investigation.

Getting on the Path to Recovery

Once the attack is contained and those who need to know have been notified, the focus shifts to recovery. Business priorities will determine which specific critical systems you bring back first, but restoring systems, data, and applications from backups is how you rebuild. But it's important to emphasize that good backups matter---they must be recent, complete, and stored so attackers can't corrupt them.

Next, you need to address the root cause---the vulnerabilities the attackers used to get in. Based on your investigation, determine the appropriate containment and eradication measures. This may involve patching vulnerabilities, removing malware, resetting passwords, or rebuilding compromised systems. Be sure to address the root cause of the breach to prevent re-occurrence.

Throughout the process, maintain clear communication and documentation. Provide regular updates to stakeholders and consider engaging external experts, such as incident response consultants or legal counsel, as needed.

Remember, the goal is not just to contain the immediate incident but also to learn from it and improve your security posture. A thorough post-mortem of the incident is crucial. What went wrong that let the attack happen in the first place? Did your incident response plan work as intended? Were communications effective? Take these hard lessons and turn them into an action plan for improving your defenses.

Conclusion

Proactive cyber incident management is a crucial part of any cyber plan. It's about being prepared, having the right tools in place, and practicing your response so that when an attack does happen, you can minimize the damage, reassure customers and partners, and quickly get your business back on track. Remember, cyber is an ongoing process---keep learning, updating, and training; your resilience against these ever-evolving threats will only grow stronger.

Answers To Key Questions

Question 1: What are the critical first steps in our incident response plan when a breach is detected?

Answer: Picture your security alarms going off - an attack is in progress! How you respond in those first chaotic moments can be the difference between a minor incident and a full-blown disaster.

Your incident response plan prioritizes three immediate actions:

First, you need to contain the threat. Think of it like quarantining a disease outbreak - you need to identify the source of the attack quickly and cut off its ability to spread further. This might involve deactivating compromised user accounts, isolating entire parts of the network to prevent attackers from moving around unnoticed, or even blocking data outflow if an exfiltration attempt is underway. Alternatively, it could be a question of isolating your systems from a compromised supplier or partner.

- ***Containment & Elimination:*** This is where having a comprehensive series of playbooks is so vital. Once the attack happens, focus on business recovery. If it's a breach through important information stolen from an employee, such as from a thumb drive, reputational management may come to the fore, as well as law enforcement and stakeholder management. If it's malware on your systems, this could mean removing any malware the attackers have installed, patching the security holes they used to get in, and disrupting their ability to control any systems they may have compromised remotely.

- ***Record Activities:*** While containment and elimination happen, the IRT must record all activities for "lessons learned." You need to understand precisely what happened, what led to the incident, and, in the case of malware, how the attackers got in, what vulnerabilities they exploited, and the extent of any data that may be compromised. This information isn't just about fixing the immediate problem - it's about strengthening your defenses so this attack can't happen again and gathering evidence in case you need to pursue legal action.

Acting swiftly and decisively across all these fronts allows us to limit the damage a breach can cause and positions you to learn from the experience, improving your overall security in the long run.

Question 2: How do we communicate clearly and effectively with stakeholders during a cyber incident?

Answer: A cyber attack isn't just about stolen data or broken systems - it creates uncertainty, and that lack of information can be as damaging as the attack itself. That's why having a clear communication plan is as important as any technical fix.

Let's start internally. When a breach happens, your employees are a primary concern. They're worried about the company's future, their data, and whether they'll have a job next week! You combat this by quickly notifying staff about the breach, even if all the details aren't yet available. This initial communication should explain what happened and the potential impact on the business and emphasize that you're actively working to contain the situation. Regular updates are critical - even if the update is "we're still investigating," it reassures people that the problem is being addressed and prevents rumors and panic from spreading. Also, designate a straightforward way for employees to ask questions - this gets reliable information flowing and heads off misinformation. Lastly, many businesses want to continue with as much of their daily operations as they can. So, a "business-as-usual" plan must also be communicated where appropriate.

Of course, you must also consider communication with external stakeholders - customers, business partners, regulators, and possibly even the media. This requires planning. Identify who might be impacted and tailor your communications to their concerns. Customers will want to know if their data was stolen, whereas a regulator needs to know the technical details of how the attack occurred. Having a spokesperson authorized to represent the company ensures a consistent message and avoids mixed signals.

Here's where things get tricky - you want to be transparent to build trust, but you can only say something that might help the attackers or reveal details of the ongoing investigation. This means carefully crafting honest communications that are not overly detailed until the immediate threat has passed.

By proactively planning communication, taking care of your employees, and tailoring your messages to external audiences, you can manage information flow effectively, minimize reputational damage, and maintain trust even during a challenging event.

Question 3: What is our strategy for recovering from a cyber attack and restoring normal operations?

Answer: Once you've contained the breach and communicated with stakeholders, your focus shifts to getting back on your feet. Here's the basic outline of your recovery plan:

Your priority is restoring business as usual. A lot depends on the nature of the attack and in which part of your ecosystem it happened. If it were your IT, contractual conversations with third parties would likely be involved in compiling a restoration plan for a malware attack. This might include using backups to replace anything damaged in the attack. Good backups are crucial - they need to be recent, complete, and stored so that attackers cannot corrupt them as well. Once you restore a data system, you must carefully check its integrity to avoid accidentally reintroducing malware into your systems.

Next, you need to "patch" the holes the attackers used to get in. In terms of a breach, this could mean changing company policies and protocols, changes to a third-party contract, and the need for specialist training. Regarding malware, your forensics team analyzes the attack to determine precisely what vulnerabilities were exploited. These get patched immediately - you don't want to leave the door open for them to return! You can also use this as an opportunity to look for any security weaknesses that the incident revealed broadly.

But recovery isn't just technical. Conduct a thorough "post-mortem" on the incident. What went wrong that let the attack happen in the first place? Did your incident response plan work? Were your communications effective? You take these hard lessons and create a detailed report on what needs to improve to prevent a similar attack in the future. This report isn't just for gathering dust - it becomes the action plan for shoring up your security moving forward.

By methodically restoring systems, patching the vulnerabilities that led to the breach, and learning every lesson from the experience, you can quickly get your operations back on track and emerge from the crisis more robust than before.

Question 4: How do we assess and improve our cyber incident response readiness?

Answer: Hoping an attack never happens isn't a strategy - you need to constantly test your readiness under realistic conditions. We suggest you use a two-part approach:

First, you run drills. These tabletop exercises or simulated attacks give your Incident Response Team (IRT) the closest thing to real-world experience without having a real-world crisis! These exercises expose weaknesses in your written response plan, let the team practice communication and coordination under pressure, and help you see where technical bottlenecks might form.

The second part is about measurement. Define key performance indicators (KPIs) that tell you how well you're prepared. Think of it like a company measuring its financial health. These metrics might track how quickly you typically detect a breach, how well your communications plan works during a drill, or how long it takes you to restore systems after a simulated attack.

Crucially, use the lessons learned from drills and your KPI tracking to improve. Maybe you discover response delays because of how your systems are configured - that's a fix you can implement. Perhaps the drills show staff confusion about reporting procedures, which needs to be addressed with training.

By actively training your team under pressure and measuring your progress, you don't just prepare to face an attack - you become more and more effective at managing it, ensuring a swift response that minimizes damage.

Question 5: What are the roles and responsibilities of our executive team during a cyber crisis?

Answer: A cyber attack isn't just a problem for the IT department - and quite often isn't - though that usually doesn't stop them from getting the blame. Fundamentally, any significant attack is a crisis for the entire business, meaning leadership needs to step up. Here's what the executive team has to do:

First and foremost, they're the decision-makers. They will need to approve how resources are shifted around to prioritize a response, sign off on communication plans so the public message is consistent, and may even need to make tough calls about acceptable risk when choosing how to respond to an attack.

But leadership isn't just about decision-making; it's about communication. When employees are scared, they look to the executives for reassurance. They need to project confidence in the company's ability to handle the crisis, communicate transparently about what's happening, and maintain morale. The executives also represent the company to the outside world—customers, regulators, and the media—and may need to act as spokespersons during the crisis.

Finally, there's the strategic side. The executive team needs to keep an eye on the big picture, ensuring resources are going where they're needed most and that the incident response team is accountable. Once the immediate crisis is over, they'll play a significant role in assessing the damage to the company's reputation and developing a long-term plan to recover and prevent future attacks.

By decisively making the tough calls, communicating in a way that inspires trust, and keeping sight of the immediate crisis and the company's long-term health, the executive team plays a critical role in turning a cyber attack from a disaster into a challenge the organization overcomes.

Question 6: How can we ensure our incident response plan is current and regularly tested?

Answer: Let's be honest: the best-laid plans can gather dust on a shelf. You need constant review and testing to keep your incident response plan battle-ready.

First, schedule regular reviews - these aren't about rewriting the whole plan every time but about ensuring it aligns with reality. New threats emerge, technologies change, and maybe you've acquired another company, and their systems need to be integrated. All these changes must be reflected in the plan, or it could steer you wrong in a crisis. You must also pull in lessons learned from your drills and attacks that have made the news. Security is an ever-evolving field, so your defenses must also evolve.

But review alone isn't enough. You must regularly run drills - everything from tabletop exercises, discussing hypothetical scenarios, to full-blown simulated attacks that test your systems and people. These drills serve multiple purposes. They let you find the gaps in your written plans. But even more importantly, they give your incident response team practice working under pressure, making decisions quickly, and communicating effectively. Like a sports team runs practice drills, this helps ensure everything goes smoothly on game day. Best practice indicates tabletop exercises should be quarterly, but an entire exercise should be run every 12-18 months.

By regularly updating and testing your security practices, you will avoid nasty surprises. When an actual attack happens, you want your response plan to be an asset, not an outdated document that leads you astray.

Question 7: How can we leverage our incident response experiences to strengthen our cyber posture?

Answer: Every breach, even if contained quickly, is a painful learning experience for an organization. The smart move is to ensure that the lessons you learn the hard way strengthen you.

Here's how to do that:

First, every past incident is like a detective story in reverse - meticulously analyze what happened to figure out how the attackers got in. This tells you which specific vulnerabilities to fix and informs what systems you need to prioritize in future security audits.

You should also look critically at how you responded to the incident. Did you detect it quickly enough? Did your communications plan work in the heat of the moment? Can you streamline any steps in your incident response plan? These answers guide you in making your detection faster, your responses more efficient, and your communications more effective the next time.

You can even use past incidents in security awareness training. Moving away from generic examples to real things that have happened in your industry or your own company helps convey to employees that these threats are real.

And perhaps most importantly, lessons learned from an incident must be incorporated into your broader incident response plan. You may need new response procedures for a specific type of attack, revised roles for your incident response team, or improved communication protocols for notifying stakeholders.

Finally, past incidents inform your threat-hunting strategies. If you see specific techniques attackers have used before, you can proactively hunt for any signs they might be trying similar things again.

By using every security incident as an opportunity to analyze, improve, and train, you transform the experience from a negative into a force that actively makes us a more challenging target in the future.

Question 8: How do we prepare for incident management's legal and public relations aspects?

Answer: A cyber attack isn't just a technical problem; it can land you in court and damage your reputation. That's why you need a plan for these aspects of crisis management.

First, there's the legal side. Get expert legal advice right away. What are your obligations if customer data is stolen? Are there regulators you need to notify? What potential fines could you face? And importantly, how must a forensics investigation be conducted to ensure evidence is admissible in court if required? Having a legal response strategy developed in advance means you're not scrambling to figure this out during a crisis.

The other half of the equation is public relations. You need a separate communications plan specifically for cyber attacks. This defines who's authorized to speak to the press - not everyone should be giving interviews! It also outlines the key messages you want to convey: that you're aware of the breach, take it seriously, and will keep the public updated. Being proactive in building relationships with relevant media outlets can also pay off when a crisis strikes - an established relationship can go a long way toward fair and accurate coverage.

By having both legal and PR response plans in place well before they're ever needed, you can minimize the reputational damage a cyber attack can cause, address your legal obligations confidently, and maintain transparency even in the most challenging situations.

Question 9: What partnerships and external resources should we have for incident management support?

Answer: No one fights alone in cyber - having the right external resources ready to help can make all the difference in the outcome of a breach. Here's why you should invest time in developing these partnerships now before a crisis hits:

First, specialized cyber firms are like bringing in reinforcements for your IT team. These companies have experts who deal with incidents day in and day out, plus they might have access to the tools we need. This extra firepower is invaluable for stopping an attack quickly and figuring out how to prevent it from happening again. Companies such as Templar Executives or F-Secure are the ideal partners for this type of situation.

You should also build relationships with law enforcement agencies specializing in cyber crime. Reporting attacks lets them track the bigger picture and even helps catch and prosecute criminals. This conveys that cyber crime isn't anonymous and can deter future attacks.

Sometimes, the aftermath of an attack requires more than your in-house IT can handle. That's where digital forensics specialists come in. They meticulously comb your systems, preserving evidence and getting a detailed attack timeline. This lets us shore up your defenses much more effectively.

Finally, don't underestimate the power of industry groups! Many have collaborative systems for sharing information about new threats, and they let you learn how other companies like yours have responded to attacks. Sometimes, attacks aren't isolated events, and working with others can give you the warning you need to get ahead of the next threat.

Establishing these relationships before you need them ensures you can quickly access your resources in a crisis. This additional support translates to faster response time, better recovery, and even the chance to gain valuable insights that prevent similar attacks in the future.

Further Reading

1. Cichonski, P., Millar, T., Grance, T., & Scarfone, K. (2012). Computer security incident handling guide (NIST Special Publication 800-61, Revision 2). National Institute of Standards and Technology. https://doi.org/10.6028/NIST.SP.800-61r2

2. Kral, P. (2011). The incident handlers handbook. SANS Institute. https://www.sans.org/reading-room/whitepapers/incident/incident-handlers-handbook-33901

3. European Union Agency for Network and Information Security. (2016). Good practice guide for incident management. https://www.enisa.europa.eu/publications/good-practice-

guide-for-incident-management

4. Menges, F., & Pernul, G. (2020). Towards a capability maturity model for incident response. Information and Computer Security, 28(3), 393-416. https://doi.org/10.1108/ICS-12-2018-0141

5. Mitropoulos, S., Patsos, D., & Douligeris, C. (2006). On incident handling and response: A state-of-the-art approach. Computers & Security, 25(5), 351-370. https://doi.org/10.1016/j.cose.2005.09.006

Chapter 10

Picking The Right Cyber Defense Tools

A robust cyber toolkit is vital for protecting critical assets and data. This chapter guides leaders and aims to help them select effective cyber defense tools that address their organization's unique needs.

The Leader's Guide to Cyber Defense Categories

Understanding the variety of cyber defense tools available is essential. For instance, endpoint security measures protect devices like desktops and mobile phones from malware and unauthorized access through tools like antivirus software and endpoint detection systems. Network security involves safeguarding your organization's infrastructure with firewalls and intrusion detection systems, crucial for preventing unauthorized access and data breaches. Data security focuses on protecting sensitive information, utilizing encryption and data loss prevention tools to secure data, whether stored in transit or in use. Security Information and Event Management (SIEM) solutions also play a pivotal role by analyzing security data from various sources to identify suspicious activity and provide timely insights. Moreover, deploying Security Orchestration, Automation, and Response (SOAR) platforms helps automate repetitive tasks, enabling analysts to concentrate on more complex threat analysis and incident responses. Platforms that gather and analyze threat intelligence data contribute significantly by offering insights into emerging threats and potential vulnerabilities.

Further dimensions include tools tailored for cloud security, becoming increasingly important as more organizations migrate to cloud-based services. Similarly, engaging security awareness training platforms helps educate employees on cyber best practices, enhancing the overall security posture.

By integrating these tools into a comprehensive security strategy, leaders can effectively address their specific security concerns and fortify their organization against cyber threats.

Strategic Questions Leaders Should Ask About Cyber Tools

Choosing the right cyber defense tools requires more than understanding different technologies; it involves strategic thinking about what the tools need to achieve. Leaders should consider which assets are crucial and must be protected at all costs. They need to identify their organization's vulnerabilities through regular assessments to ensure the chosen tools can effectively address these weak points. Compliance with industry regulations and maintaining a realistic budget for cyber are also critical. Furthermore, the compatibility of new tools with existing IT infrastructures, the expertise available among staff members, the scalability of the tools to accommodate future growth, and the level of vendor support must all be considered to ensure effective implementation and operation.

Balancing Cost and Value in Cyber Investments

Balancing the cost and value of cyber investments is crucial. Prioritizing preventative tools can significantly reduce the likelihood and impact of cyber attacks, potentially saving on expensive recovery efforts. Integrating and automating security tools can enhance efficiency and reduce the chances of human error. Leaders should weigh the benefits of open-source tools against commercial solutions, which offer more support despite potentially higher costs. Cloud-based solutions often provide scalability and reduce the need for significant initial investments. Leaders are advised to take advantage of free trials and proofs of concept to assess tool effectiveness before committing fully. They should also consider the total cost of ownership, including the purchase price and ongoing maintenance and training expenses. However, when designing new systems, everyone should think that "secure by design" is the most cost-effective way of investing.

Integration with existing Systems

Effective implementation and change management are critical to the success of any new security tool. Start by clearly defining the tool's objectives and benefits and how it aligns with your overall security strategy. Engage key stakeholders from across the organization (e.g., IT, operations, legal) early to gather requirements and build buy-in.

Develop a comprehensive project plan that includes milestones, responsibilities, and contingencies. Communicate the plan widely and provide regular updates on progress and challenges.

Conduct thorough testing before widely deploying the tool. This should include technical and user acceptance testing to ensure the tool integrates smoothly with existing workflows. Provide ample training and support during the rollout, and consider a phased approach to allow for learning and adjustment.

Establish clear metrics to measure the tool's effectiveness and adoption. Regularly collect and act on user feedback. Celebrate successes and quickly address any issues that arise.

Remember, effective change management is an ongoing process. Continue to invest in training, communication, and refinement to ensure the tool delivers maximum value over time.

Conclusion

In conclusion, selecting appropriate cyber defense tools involves carefully analyzing your organization's needs, strategic planning, and balancing cost and value. By understanding the various categories of tools, ensuring they align with your specific requirements, and investing wisely, leaders can secure their organizations against current and evolving cyber threats. This strategic approach and continuous investment in technology and staff training are essential for maintaining robust cyber defenses and ensuring business continuity in a digital world.

Answers To Key Questions

Question 1: What are the primary categories of cyber defense tools, and how do they differ in functionality and protection level?

Answer: Think of cyber defense as a layered system with various tools tackling different parts of the problem. Endpoint security is like having a guard at every door and window of your house - it protects individual computers and devices from malware, phishing attempts, and unauthorized access. Meanwhile, network security is like the walls and gates around your property, with firewalls, intrusion detection systems, and network segmentation tools keeping intruders out and segmenting your network to contain any threat that does slip through.

Data security focuses on your most valuable assets. Encryption scrambles information so it's useless to an attacker, while data loss prevention tools stop leaks and data classification software helps you track where the most sensitive information is stored.

Other tools focus on the bigger picture. Security Information and Event Management (SIEM) systems gather data from your whole security setup, flagging unusual activity and giving you a central place to look for threats. Security Orchestration, Automation, and Response (SOAR) platforms reduce the workload on security teams by automating repetitive tasks, freeing them up to investigate complex threats. Finally, threat intelligence platforms track broader trends, letting you anticipate what attackers are likely to try next.

Combining these different categories creates multiple barriers that an attacker must break through - a far more effective strategy than relying on any one tool.

Question 2: How do these categories of cyber defense tools align with our current organizational structure and existing security protocols?

Answer: Figuring out where new tools fit isn't just about strategic fit - even if viewed through the classic strategic lenses of technology, people, and processes. It is about getting the right fit in terms of usability, adoption, and engagement. Start by understanding your security landscape. Who is currently responsible for various security tasks - is this just IT, or do departments like HR or legal have defined roles? Is a formal governance structure in place, and what part do appointed roles play? Next, examine what each department already does to stay secure: Do they have access control procedures? What are their plans for responding to an incident?

Once you know the "who" and the "how" of your existing security, it's easier to see where tools bring value. Maybe your access control policies are well-defined, but manually enforcing them is a nightmare - this signals a good use case for a Data Loss Prevention (DLP) tool. Likewise, if your incident response plans are thorough but slow, a Security Orchestration, Automation, and Response (SOAR) platform could streamline the process, getting problems fixed faster.

This analysis isn't just about plugging gaps! It also highlights where tools can make existing procedures far more powerful. This approach gives you a double benefit: more robust overall security and a better return on your investment in any new technology. Remember, a "secure by design" approach is critical to success.

Question 3: Given our industry and threat landscape, are there any new or emerging categories of cyber defense tools that we should be aware of?

Answer: Certainly. As cyber threats evolve, so too must our defensive strategies. Several emerging categories of tools warrant consideration.

Firstly, the cyber domain is highly specialized, with attackers exploiting the unique vulnerabilities of various sectors. To effectively counter these threats, it's essential to invest in tools designed to address the specific challenges faced by your industry. These tools have a deeper understanding of common attack vectors and offer the tailored protection your organization needs.

Secondly, cloud-based security solutions offer the key advantages of scalability and ease of management. They can seamlessly adapt to your organization's changing needs, and their centralized nature simplifies administration for your IT teams.

Finally, consider incorporating deception technology into your defensive strategy. This proactive approach deploys decoys and honeypots within your network, misleading attackers and diverting them from critical systems. Deception technology can be a powerful tool, buying valuable time to identify and neutralize genuine threats.

The continuous evolution of cyber threats necessitates a proactive and agile approach to defense. Understanding your organization's specific vulnerabilities and exploring the latest advancements in security technology will significantly strengthen your defensive posture. Lastly, don't forget about people. External geopolitical events and social media trends espousing misinformation and disinformation can motivate destructive behaviors or induce insider threats. Organizations must maintain an agile posture to reflect the changing threat environment.

Question 4: What specific cyber threats are our biggest concerns, and which tools are best suited to mitigate these risks?

Answer: Pinpointing your organization's most significant cyber threats is like playing a high-stakes game of chess - every move must be strategic and focused on protecting what matters most.

To start, you need to understand the battlefield. Study the types of attacks common in your industry and identify any weak points in your defenses that might tempt an attacker. Once you have this threat assessment, carefully prioritize the risks. Some attacks might be more likely, while others could cause more significant damage if successful. That prioritization is your guidebook for choosing your weapons.

Each type of cyber attack has its own set of countermeasures. If phishing scams are your biggest worry, consider tools that protect individual devices and detect and block malicious emails before they do damage. On the other hand, if you're most concerned about data leaks, investigate tools that safeguard your most sensitive information by strictly controlling who can access it and how.

This targeted approach is the key to efficiency in cyber. You'll create a robust, focused defense that protects your vital assets from harm by focusing your resources on the tools that directly address your organization's most pressing threats.

Question 5: How do the cyber tools we are considering integrate with our existing systems and security measures?

Answer: Think of your cyber setup like an orchestra. Each instrument has a vital role, but the orchestra only makes beautiful music if all the instruments play in harmony. The same goes for your security tools. Seamless integration is essential for maximizing their effectiveness and making your IT team's life easier.

Firstly, you'll want to picture your entire security ecosystem. How will the new tool fit in with your current firewalls, intrusion detection systems, and the platform that collects and analyzes security events? The best tools are designed to play well with others.

Secondly, look for the "common language" of cyber. Industry-standard protocols allow different tools to talk to each other, sharing information and triggering actions without friction. The more standardized the communication, the smoother the integration.

Finally, consider compatibility. Double-check that your potential new tool is compatible with your current operating system, hardware, and essential software applications. Nobody wants to discover a glaring incompatibility after investing in the technology.

Focusing on integration will create a streamlined and efficient security setup. Your tools will work in concert, providing a robust defense that's more than the sum of its parts.

Question 6: Can the tools scale with our business growth and adapt to evolving cyber threats?

Answer: In the world of cyber, standing still means falling behind. Not only do you need tools to handle today's threats, but they also need to grow and change with your business to protect you against tomorrow's attacks.

First, think about scalability. Picture your organization doubling or even tripling in size. Will your chosen cyber tools be able to keep up? Look for solutions with flexible licensing models or hosted in the cloud. These can seamlessly expand as your needs grow without requiring a complete overhaul of your defenses.

Next, consider adaptability. Cyber criminals are constantly refining their tactics and finding new ways to exploit vulnerabilities. The tools you choose should be able to learn and evolve alongside them, drawing on up-to-date threat intelligence and utilizing techniques like machine learning to spot suspicious behavior patterns.

Investing in cyber is about more than solving today's problems. By choosing tools designed for scale and adaptability, you're building a defensive strategy that will protect your organization now and well into the future.

Question 7: How do we measure the ROI of cyber investments, and how does this influence our decision-making process for selecting cyber defense tools?

Answer: Cyber isn't like buying a new machine that produces more widgets - -the benefits aren't always tangible. That said, the cost of not investing in security can be astronomical. The trick is understanding the delicate balance between the cost of your tools and the potential cost of the attacks they prevent.

Imagine the worst-case scenario: a severe data breach, a system-wide shutdown, or even reputational harm leading to lost customers. Estimate the financial hit your business could take in any of these situations. Now, compare that to the cost of the cyber tools you're considering. This gives you a ballpark idea of the potential savings of a robust security posture.

Of course, prevention is hard to quantify. You can't put an exact dollar figure on a phishing attack that didn't happen. That's where tracking improvement comes in. Keep a close eye on crucial security metrics: Are your email filters blocking more suspicious attempts? Are vulnerability scans finding fewer weaknesses? These positive trends indicate that your tools are working and saving money, even if they aren't directly making you money.

Armed with this knowledge, your decision-making becomes much more straightforward. Cost isn't the only factor, but you can make informed choices based on the potential financial risk a given tool mitigates and its proven ability to bolster your defenses.

Question 8: What is the balance between the cost of these tools and their value in risk mitigation and business continuity?

Answer: Think of cyber spending like an insurance policy. If something goes wrong, you pay a premium to offset a much steeper cost. But just like with insurance, you want to ensure you get the best coverage for your money.

Focus on prevention first. Measures and tools that stop attacks at the source, such as a proactive governance structure, robust endpoint security, a well-guarded network, and regular employee training, reduce the chances you'll ever have to deal with a costly breach or system outage.

Next, do your research. Compare features carefully against the upfront price and ongoing costs like licensing and maintenance within any tool category. Look beyond the sticker price and consider the "total cost of ownership" over time. A slightly more expensive tool can save you money in the long run if it's easier to use or more effective at blocking threats.

But technology isn't everything. Your best security tool is a well-informed workforce. Invest in security awareness programs that teach employees to spot and avoid dangers like phishing emails. A robust human firewall is a cost-effective way to enhance the value of any technology you purchase.

It's also essential to consider your IT team's expertise. The most sophisticated tools in the world are only helpful if people know how to use them properly. Support your security team with training and development so they can get the most out of your cyber investments.

Finding the right balance can be challenging. But by approaching your choices strategically and focusing on the tools and the people who use them, you'll create a security strategy that protects your business without breaking the bank.

Question 9: What are the financial implications of a potential breach compared to investing in these cyber defense tools?

Answer: Imagine trying to put a price tag on a nightmare. That's what you're doing when considering the cost of a data breach. Beyond the immediate expenses - the forensics experts, the lawyers, the regulatory fines - you have the hidden costs that can linger for years: lost business, damaged reputation, and lingering mistrust among your customers.

The scary truth is that the price of a breach can dwarf the cost of the best cyber tools on the market. It's a gamble no business can afford to take.

Think of cyber investment like preventative medicine. Yes, there's an upfront cost. But by taking steps to protect your systems, train your people, and be vigilant against the latest threats, you have a much better chance of sidestepping the kind of catastrophe that could cripple your business financially.

A robust cyber posture isn't about buying peace of mind - though that's certainly valuable. It's about sound business sense. The decision becomes clear by weighing the relatively small investment in prevention against the astronomical potential costs of a breach. This isn't an optional expense; it's an investment in your company's survival.

Further Reading

1. National Institute of Standards and Technology. (2017). NIST special publication 800-53, revision 5: Security and privacy controls for information systems and organizations. https://doi.org/10.6028/NIST.SP.800-53r5

2. Scarfone, K., & Souppaya, M. (2012). Guide to enterprise patch management technologies (NIST Special Publication 800-40, Revision 3). National Institute of Standards and Technology. https://doi.org/10.6028/NIST.SP.800-40r3

3. Sedgewick, A., Souppaya, M., & Scarfone, K. (2015). Guide to application whitelisting (NIST Special Publication 800-167). National Institute of Standards and Technology. https://doi.org/10.6028/NIST.SP.800-167

4. Cser, A., Balaouras, S., & McClean, C. (2020). The Forrester Wave™: Security analytics platforms, Q4 2020. Forrester Research. https://www.forrester.com/report/The-Forrester-Wave-Security-Analytics-Platforms-Q4-2020/RES161187

5. Chuvakin, A., & Barros, A. (2019). 2020 SANS cyber threat intelligence (CTI) survey. SANS Institute. https://www.sans.org/reading-room/whitepapers/threats/2020-cyber-threat-

Chapter 11

Secure Innovation As A Competitive Advantage

In the past, cyber might have been seen as a hindrance to innovation - a necessary cost that slowed progress. But today's most successful organizations have flipped this script. They understand that robust security isn't an afterthought but the foundation for lasting innovation. In a world where data breaches and cyber attacks make constant headlines, a reputation for strong security is a currency that translates directly into customer trust and market dominance.

Microsoft's transformation into a cyber titan offers a compelling example. By investing massively in securing its suite of products and cloud services, the company has earned the confidence of enterprise clients worldwide. This reputation for security has helped Microsoft secure massive contracts, often edging out competitors with less robust cyber postures.

Similarly, other companies like American Express have established themselves as champions of data security, especially within the notoriously risk-conscious financial sector. For decades, the company has invested heavily in protecting customer information, fostering a sense of deep loyalty among cardholders. Their commitment to security extends beyond compliance, enhancing its reputation as an industry leader dedicated to customer protection.

Technology pioneers like Intel showcase the wisdom of integrating security into every stage of product development. Their "secure by design" approach goes beyond simply adding security features at the end of the development cycle. Instead, security has been a guiding principle since day one, ensuring new releases aren't just innovative and resilient to ever-evolving cyber threats. This proactive strategy saves time and money by reducing the need for expensive security reworks later in development. Even agile tech startups embrace this mindset, often incorporating "security sprints" into their development cycles to ensure that each release maintains functionality and robust security.

Building a culture of secure innovation requires strong leadership. It's no coincidence that companies known for their commitment to cyber often have vocal advocates at the helm. Executives like Satya Nadella at Microsoft have repeatedly and publicly championed integrating security into all aspects of the business. They understand cyber isn't merely an IT concern but a core element of every product, service, and decision. Similarly, Cisco's leadership team emphasizes the question "How secure?" alongside the traditional "what?" and "how?" This approach trickles down throughout the organization, ensuring security is at the forefront of innovation from brainstorming to project launch.

Aligning Cyber with Business Expansion

As businesses grow and evolve, their cyber strategies must adapt accordingly to address new risks and vulnerabilities. Shopify's meteoric growth in the e-commerce sector offers a powerful case study. To support its rapidly expanding network of online merchants and shoppers, its security architecture has had to evolve in tandem, utilizing sophisticated fraud detection and data protection strategies to keep pace with the growth.

Strategic partnerships and acquisitions also demand meticulous cyber planning. Before engaging in collaboration, companies must conduct rigorous due diligence to evaluate the security posture of potential partners. This step is necessary to protect your organization, as interconnected systems increase your attack surface. Smart collaborations require data-sharing protocols, careful system integration, and a shared commitment to proactive security that addresses the needs of all parties involved.

Finally, cyber must be a core consideration during expansions into new markets or developing new products and services. Consider traditional banks venturing into the world of mobile banking. While innovative, this new service sector presents an expanded cyber challenge. Mobile devices represent a new potential vulnerability, requiring extra vigilance in protecting sensitive customer financial data. Anticipating and mitigating these challenges before launch is the only way to ensure a smooth and secure expansion.

Fostering a Secure Innovation Ecosystem

Building a genuinely secure innovation ecosystem demands more than investing in the right tools and technologies. It requires a fundamental cultural shift within your organization - a shift from reactive firefighting to proactive security-mindedness. Here's how to cultivate that mindset:

- *Invest in Ongoing Security Awareness Training:* Knowledge is power, but only if it's applied. That's why ongoing security awareness training for your entire workforce is non-negotiable. This isn't just about IT staff - developers, product managers, and even executives must understand cyber best practices, the threats targeting your industry, and their roles in safeguarding your company's innovations.

  Think of this training as building armor suits tailored to each person's specific role. Developers need in-depth training on secure coding practices, the types of vulnerabilities attackers exploit, and how to use secure coding tools. Product managers should learn to think like attackers, understanding how seemingly innocuous product features or user workflows could create exploitable weaknesses. Executives need a high-level understanding of the threat landscape, the costs of a breach (both financial and reputational), and the importance of treating cyber as a business-critical investment.

Ditch the boring lectures! Interactive training methods are far more effective in changing behaviors. Gamify the process with simulated cyber scenarios, role-playing exercises, and even competitions to promote both knowledge and vigilance within your company.

- ***Embrace DevSecOps***

    - DevSecOps is more than just a buzzword - it's about weaving security into the fabric of your software development lifecycle. Foster collaboration between developers, security teams, and operations personnel to catch vulnerabilities before they become expensive problems.

    - The mantra of DevSecOps is "shifting security left." This means moving testing and vulnerability identification to the beginning of the development process, not just tacking it on at the end. This saves time, money, and headaches by allowing developers to fix security flaws as they code rather than scrambling to patch vulnerabilities in a finished product.

    - Automation is your friend. Invest in DevSecOps tools that automate code scanning, identify weaknesses in your infrastructure, and conduct security assessments throughout the development journey. By automating these tedious tasks, developers can focus on their primary job - building innovative features - with the peace of mind that security is simultaneously baked into their work.

    - Integrating security into agile development

methodologies requires shifting from traditional, linear approaches to a more iterative and collaborative model. Start by establishing a shared understanding of security requirements and risks among all development team members, including business owners, developers, and testers.

- Incorporate security user stories and acceptance criteria into each sprint alongside functional requirements. This ensures that security considerations are baked into each feature from the start rather than bolted on at the end.

- Implement secure coding practices and provide developers with ongoing training and tools to identify and remediate vulnerabilities early in development. Use automated security testing tools, such as static code analysis and dependency scanning, to catch issues as soon as they're introduced.

- Regular security reviews and penetration tests should be conducted throughout the development lifecycle, not just before release. Integrate these findings back into the backlog for prioritization and remediation.

- Foster a culture of continuous improvement and learning. Encourage developers to take ownership of security and provide them with the resources and support they need to do so effectively.

- By embedding security into each iteration and making it a shared responsibility of the entire team, organizations can keep pace with rapid innovation while ensuring a strong security posture.

- ***Plan for a different technical future.*** As organizations rush to adopt emerging technologies like AI, blockchain, and quantum computing, it's crucial to address each technology's unique security implications proactively.

- For AI systems, key considerations include ensuring the integrity and security of training data, protecting against malicious inputs or model poisoning attacks, and maintaining transparency and accountability in decision-making processes. Organizations should implement robust data governance practices, regularly audit and test AI models for vulnerabilities, and establish ethical guidelines for AI development and deployment.

- With blockchain, while the underlying technology is designed to be secure and immutable, vulnerabilities can still arise in the smart contracts and applications built on top of it. Organizations should conduct thorough code reviews and security audits of all blockchain-based systems and stay up-to-date with emerging best practices for secure blockchain development.

- Quantum computing poses a long-term challenge to many existing cryptographic systems. Organizations should start planning for "quantum-resistant" or "post-quantum" cryptography and stay abreast of ongoing research and standards development.

- More broadly, organizations should approach emerging technologies with a security-first mindset. This means conducting thorough risk assessments before adoption, establishing precise security requirements and architectural principles, and building security into the design and implementation of these systems from the ground up.

- It also means investing in the skills and knowledge needed to securely deploy and manage these technologies. This may require specialized training for developers and security teams and ongoing collaboration with external experts and research organizations.

- *Tap into the Power of Bug Bounties.* Consider setting up a bug bounty program to harness the power of ethical hackers. These programs incentivize security researchers to uncover flaws in your products or services. Think of it as hiring an elite team of testers, constantly probing your defenses to find vulnerabilities before malicious actors do. A successful bug bounty program requires careful planning. Clearly define its scope: what vulnerabilities are you looking for, and what's off-limits? Determine appropriate reward tiers based on the criticality of the issues discovered. Most importantly, trust with ethical hackers can be built by communicating, responding promptly to reported vulnerabilities, and acknowledging the value of their contributions.

Beyond Tech: People Are Key to Security

From the Board down, create a proactive governance structure with clear roles and responsibilities identified to manage risks within the Board's strategic Risk Appetite. Identify and empower "security champions" within different departments of your organization. These enthusiastic individuals can promote a security-conscious culture among their colleagues as a vital bridge between developers and your dedicated security team. Look for employees across the company who are passionate about security, have strong communication skills, and thrive on a collaborative approach. Provide them the training and resources to become effective advocates for a secure development mindset within their teams.

Open communication is crucial. Foster an environment where employees feel comfortable reporting potential security weaknesses or suspicious activity without fear of blame. Make the reporting process crystal clear, and ensure your team knows that early warning of a problem is the most valuable information.

Reward secure behavior. Establish clear security metrics for relevant teams and integrate these metrics into performance evaluations. Track the number of identified and fixed vulnerabilities, the speed of incident response, or completion rates for security training modules. By tying good security behavior directly to employee evaluations, you solidify its importance within the company culture.

Finally, share threat intelligence. Promote the sharing of valuable information on the latest threats and attack methods within your organization and, when appropriate, with industry partners or trusted Information Sharing and Analysis Centers (ISACs). Think of threat intelligence as the shared radar network of the cyber world; by pooling knowledge, everyone becomes better protected.

The Bottom Line

Building a culture of secure innovation isn't a quick fix. It's an ongoing process requiring investment in your technology and your people. By engaging in security education, integrating secure practices into everyday development with DevSecOps, and empowering employees to act as security champions, you build a resilient, innovative organization that attackers will find far less appealing to target.

Answers To Key Questions

Question 1: How can we leverage cyber as a competitive advantage in our innovation strategies?

Answer: Cyber isn't just about mitigating risk - it's a powerful business tool. Customers, partners, and investors are increasingly demanding secure solutions. Proactive security isn't just a cost center; it's a way to stand out from competitors and open new doors.

Imagine launching a new product that handles sensitive data. Potential clients will think twice if they have doubts about your security practices. A reputation for taking security seriously puts you ahead of the pack. It demonstrates reliability and instils the trust that's vital for building strong relationships.

Furthermore, prioritizing security throughout the design process can streamline innovation. Instead of scrambling to fix vulnerabilities late in the game, your team can proactively address them, potentially preventing costly delays. A security-first approach can even lead to new product features that enhance customer appeal.

You gain a serious competitive advantage by defining cyber as an essential and innovative part of your business. Clients and partners will see you as a reliable, forward-thinking company committed to protecting their data and your reputation.

Question 2: What are the best practices for balancing rapid innovation and robust security?

Answer: It's tempting to consider security a roadblock to innovation. The reality is quite the opposite. Here's how to strike the right balance:

Start by changing the mindset within your organization. Security shouldn't be an afterthought tacked onto a finished product. Embed security-conscious thinking into every step of the development process. This means training engineers on secure coding practices, threat modeling, and the importance of building security safeguards directly into new features.

Think of it like building a house - you don't just install an alarm system at the end; you consider security when laying the foundation. By taking a proactive approach, you avoid the need for rushed, makeshift solutions down the line that could compromise innovation or create new risks.

Adopting a "DevSecOps" approach is crucial. This means integrating security practices seamlessly alongside development and operations. Encourage collaboration between security teams and developers, fostering a shared understanding of security goals and potential threats within the context of the innovation process.

Automation is also crucial. Incorporate tools that automatically scan code for vulnerabilities, test for security issues, and enforce security policies. This allows your team to innovate quickly without sacrificing security.

Remember, security and innovation aren't enemies - they're partners. By baking security into every stage of the innovation process, you create products that are both cutting-edge and trustworthy.

Question 3: How can our cyber measures enhance customer trust and brand reputation?

Answer: A reputation for solid cyber translates directly into customer trust and brand loyalty. Proactive security demonstrates that the protection of customer data is a top priority. It tells the world that your company is vigilant against vulnerabilities, ensuring that the information entrusted to you is secure.

This reputation can be further enhanced by prioritizing transparency. Communicating your security measures to your customer base without resorting to overly technical jargon reinforces a sense of trust and sophistication. Customers become confident not only in your security practices but also in your commitment to open communication.

Neglecting cyber is an invitation to disaster. Data breaches and security lapses severely damage customer confidence and long-term brand health. Investing in a robust security posture and communicating those efforts effectively is a strategy that protects your customers, builds trust, and solidifies your company's reputation as a reliable industry leader.

Ultimately, customers want to do business with companies they can trust. By demonstrating that you take the safety of their data seriously, you're not just protecting your business - you're building a loyal customer base that knows they can rely on you.

Question 4: As we expand our business, what strategic steps should we take to ensure our cyber measures scale accordingly?

Answer: Growth is exciting, but it also creates new cyber challenges. As your digital footprint expands, you must ensure your defenses don't fall behind. Here's a strategic approach to ensure your security posture scales along with your business:

Begin by reassessing your threat landscape. As your operations grow, you become a bigger target for cyber criminals. Identify the new vulnerabilities that come with expanded data storage, increased user accounts, and potentially complex new systems.

Focus on flexibility and standardization. Look for security solutions with flexible licensing models that integrate smoothly into your existing infrastructure as it grows. Standardized protocols and tools across your organization streamline management and make security more scalable.

Consider a cloud-first approach. Cloud-based security can scale effortlessly with your business, eliminating the need for significant hardware investments and simplifying deployment as your needs change. Of course, cloud security has its own unique considerations and needs to be carefully evaluated.

Remember the human element. Invest in ongoing security awareness training for all employees, including new hires. As your team grows, so does the potential for human error. A security-conscious workforce is your most robust line of defense, regardless of your company's size.

Finally, proactive threat monitoring is crucial. Solutions that provide real-time visibility into your network are essential to spotting and thwarting attacks quickly. These tools should handle increasing traffic volumes as your business expands.

Remember, cyber isn't a one-time project - it's a journey that evolves alongside your business. By strategically planning for growth and prioritizing scalability, you'll create a security strategy that safeguards your business from day one to Initial

Public Offering (IPO) and beyond.

Question 5: How can we ensure our cyber strategy aligns with our business objectives and expansion plans?

Answer: Cyber isn't an isolated concern - it needs to be woven into the fabric of your business strategy. Treating it as an afterthought invites costly risks and potential roadblocks. Here's how to create alignment:

Firstly, understand that your cyber needs will evolve alongside your business. Expanding into new markets might mean complying with different data regulations, and launching new products could introduce new technical vulnerabilities to address. Anticipate these changes and proactively adjust your security plan to mitigate risks.

Involve stakeholders from across the business in cyber discussions. Security isn't just an IT problem. Input from product development, marketing, and HR will help you pinpoint potential risks and identify areas where security measures can directly support innovation and growth.

Foster a culture of "security by design." Instead of reacting to threats, train developers to consider data protection and system resiliency at every stage of product development. This proactive approach streamlines operations, prevents costly redesigns, and enhances your company's reputation.

Regularly review and update your cyber plan with business expansion in mind. Consider your growth projections: will you be handling larger volumes of sensitive data? Entering regulated industries? Expanding internationally? Align your security strategy with these milestones to ensure a smooth and secure transition.

Remember, cyber can be a powerful growth enabler. A robust plan lets you confidently take on exciting new ventures, knowing your assets are protected. By treating cyber as an integral part of your business strategy, you'll create an innovative and resilient company ready for whatever the future brings.

Question 6: What are the potential cyber risks associated with new market entry, and how can we mitigate them proactively?

Answer: Venturing into new markets is thrilling, but it's a journey that demands extra cyber vigilance. New markets often mean unfamiliar threat actors, differing legal requirements, and a growing network infrastructure that can expose you to more risk. Here's how to fortify your defenses:

Start with thorough due diligence. Research the cyber landscape of the new market. Understand the prevalent threats targeting businesses in your sector and identify any regulatory or compliance requirements specific to handling data in that region. Don't make assumptions - ignorance is costly.

Localize your security plan. Blanket cyber strategies won't cut it. You'll need to tailor your approach to the specific threats and regulations of the new market. Consider partnering with a security consultancy specializing in that region for deeper insights and tailored guidance.

Protect your expanding infrastructure. As you set up new offices and networks or partner with local vendors, enforce your security standards immediately. Inconsistencies create vulnerabilities that opportunistic attackers will exploit.

Extend your vigilance to third parties. Carefully screen new vendors and partners in the target market. Ensure their security practices align with yours, as their vulnerabilities can quickly become yours. Contractual agreements should clearly outline security responsibilities to avoid disastrous surprises.

Finally, don't forget your most valuable asset - your employees. Provide focused security training for staff operating in or frequently interacting with the new market. Educate them about the specific local threats and how to spot and report suspicious activity.

Proactive mitigation is far cheaper than damage control. Entering a new market with robust and targeted cyber measures shows your preparedness, reduces costly surprises, and ensures that your expansion is secure from the start.

Question 7: How can we foster a culture of secure innovation among our employees, partners, and suppliers?

Answer: Building a culture of secure innovation isn't about policing people - it's about empowering them. Your goal is to create an environment where everyone feels invested in your company's innovative spirit and the security of its assets. Here's how to achieve that:

Lead from the top. Senior leadership must consistently communicate the priority of security within the context of innovation. Security can't be seen as a roadblock to progress but as part of responsible and forward-thinking development.

Make security accessible. Security training can't be a series of boring presentations or jargon-filled documents that people ignore. Training should be engaging, tailored to different roles, and focused on the specific threats relevant to your business. Compliance becomes second nature when employees understand the "why" behind security measures.

Gamify security whenever possible. Turn security awareness into a challenge, with rewards for reporting vulnerabilities or excellent security practices. A little healthy competition can turn vigilance into a habit that benefits everyone.

Encourage open communication. Build channels where employees can quickly raise security concerns without fear of blame or reprisal. When everyone feels empowered to speak up, you catch potential problems before they become disasters.

Extend your culture to partners and suppliers. Don't be afraid to set security expectations as part of any vendor or partnership agreement. Offer resources and training to help them meet your standards and make clear that their security practices impact your business directly.

Most importantly, celebrate success. Make it known when a vulnerability is proactively found, or an attack is thwarted due to employee vigilance. Positive reinforcement is a powerful motivator for maintaining a security-focused mindset.

Remember, a culture of secure innovation isn't built overnight. But by prioritizing engagement, education, and clear communication, you can protect your organization and allow innovation to flourish without unnecessary risk.

Question 8: What role do training and awareness play in maintaining a secure innovation ecosystem, and how can we measure their effectiveness?

Answer: Training and awareness are the cornerstones of a secure innovation ecosystem. Think of them as the armor your employees, partners, and suppliers wear in the ever-evolving battle against cyber threats. Here's why they're vital and how to ensure your efforts pay off:

Training turns knowledge into power. Employees can't defend against threats they don't understand. Regular training on topics like secure coding practices, phishing scams, and recognizing social engineering tactics empowers everyone to make smarter security choices in their daily work.

Awareness builds vigilance. Knowing about a threat doesn't mean people will actively look out for it. Ongoing awareness campaigns, from posters to simulated phishing attacks, keep security top-of-mind. It's like putting up "look both ways" signs--a constant reminder makes safe habits instinctive.

But are you getting your money's worth? Measuring the effectiveness of these initiatives is critical. Here's how:

Track metrics before and after training. Do phishing click-through rates drop significantly after a targeted training session? That's a good sign people are internalizing the lessons learned.

Conduct simulated attacks---stage ethical "social engineering" or phishing attempts to test your workforce. Analyzing the response helps identify areas where better training or awareness reinforcement is needed.

Encourage reporting. Track the number of potential security incidents reported by employees. An uptick indicates a more alert and engaged workforce.

Security training isn't about passing a test but creating long-term behavioral shifts. By combining engaging training, constant awareness building, and a commitment to measuring results, you'll empower your team to be your innovation ecosystem's first line of defense.

Question 9: What are the best ways to engage and collaborate with external stakeholders (e.g., industry groups and regulatory bodies) to enhance our cyber posture in the context of innovation?

Answer: No organization is an island in the complex and ever-evolving world of cyber . Engaging with external stakeholders is critical to staying ahead of the curve, strengthening defenses, and fueling innovation while managing risk. Here's how to maximize the value of these collaborations:

Join forces with industry groups. Sector-specific organizations offer a wealth of shared knowledge about the latest threats, vulnerabilities, and best practices tailored to your industry. These groups often provide access to resources, tools, and insights you wouldn't have on your own.

Collaborate with regulatory bodies. While compliance can feel like a burden, proactive engagement with regulators can be a strategic asset. Understand their priorities, share your challenges, and work together to develop solutions that enhance both security and innovation. Being at the table shapes the conversation.

Participate in information-sharing networks. Threat intelligence sharing, such as through Information Sharing and Analysis Centers (ISACs), provides real-time insights into emerging threats. By contributing to and drawing from this collective knowledge pool, you strengthen your defenses and those of your peers.

Engage in public-private partnerships. Collaborations between government agencies, academia, and the private sector can drive powerful cyber innovations. These partnerships provide access to cutting-edge research, specialized expertise, and even funding opportunities.

Leverage managed security services. For specific needs, engaging with a managed security service provider (MSSP) can provide specialized expertise and scalable resources. MSSPs can help fill gaps in your in-house capabilities and provide valuable external perspectives on your security posture.

Remember, cyber is a team sport. By actively engaging with external stakeholders, you tap into a powerful network of knowledge, resources, and support. These collaborations not only strengthen your own defenses but also contribute to the collective resilience of your industry and the wider business community.

Further Reading

1. Schilling, M. A. (2017). Strategic management of technological innovation (5th ed.). McGraw-Hill Education.

2. Utterback, J. M., & Abernathy, W. J. (1975). A dynamic model of process and product innovation. Omega, 3(6), 639-656. https://doi.org/10.1016/0305-0483(75)90068-7

3. Christensen, C. M. (2013). The innovator's dilemma: When new technologies cause great firms to fail. Harvard Business Review Press.

4. Gundert, L., & Ulmer, G. (2022). The privacy engineer's manifesto: Getting from policy to code to QA to value (2nd ed.). Apress. https://doi.org/10.1007/978-1-4842-8395-1

5. Miller, D., & Proctor, A. (2016). Enterprise cyber study guide: How to build a successful cyberdefense program against advanced threats. Apress. https://doi.org/10.1007/978-1-4842-2184-1

Chapter 12

Shaping Your Future Cyber Success

In the current tempestuous geopolitical landscape, cyber threats are increasing significantly. Navigating this complex environment may seem challenging for a business leader, but this chapter will provide you with the knowledge and strategies to proactively secure your organization's future. We will explore key concepts and practical approaches clearly and engagingly.

Embracing Change: Cyber in the Age of Acceleration

The cyber environment is fast-paced, with cyber criminals continuously developing new attack methods, requiring businesses to adopt a culture of continuous adaptation. While the rapid advancement of technology presents challenges, it also brings innovative solutions. Artificial Intelligence (AI) can analyze large data sets to identify patterns and predict potential attacks, acting as tireless security analysts. Automation in cyber can streamline repetitive tasks, such as patching vulnerabilities and detecting suspicious activities, enhancing efficiency and reducing human errors. Cloud-based security solutions provide flexibility and scalability, allowing businesses to adapt their security measures as they grow without significant investment in physical infrastructure. By utilizing these technologies, companies can transition from a reactive to a proactive security stance, anticipating and preventing threats before they occur.

Cultivating a Proactive Cyber Mindset

A proactive cyber approach involves continuously strengthening an organization's defenses, training employees, and maintaining vigilance. It begins with establishing a board-level governance structure to proactively manage cyber risk and empower employees through regular security awareness training. This education helps employees recognize and avoid potential threats, such as phishing emails, equipping them with the tools to contribute to the organization's security. Penetration testing, or ethical hacking, is another proactive measure where security professionals simulate attacks to identify and address vulnerabilities. This proactive identification is preferable to reacting to an actual exploited weakness. Furthermore, a well-defined incident response plan prepares your organization to act quickly and effectively if a breach occurs, minimizing potential damage and downtime.

Take the Long-term View.

Given the constantly evolving threat landscape, long-term budgeting and resource allocation for cyber initiatives can be challenging. However, some fundamental principles can help leaders ensure adequate and sustained investment.

Start by treating cyber as a core business function, not just an IT cost center. Engage business leaders in the budgeting process to ensure that security investments align with the company's overall strategy and risk management priorities.

Use risk-based budgeting to prioritize investments based on different threats' likelihood and potential impact. This ensures that limited resources are focused on the areas of greatest need.

Build flexibility into budgets by allocating a portion of funds for emergent needs or unexpected incidents. Consider establishing a dedicated cyber reserve fund that can be used in case of a significant breach or to take advantage of new opportunities.

Advocate for sustained, multi-year funding rather than just annual budgets. This provides greater predictability and allows for longer-term planning and more strategic initiatives.

Benchmark your spending regularly against industry peers and best practices to ensure you are keeping pace with evolving standards. Engage third-party experts to conduct periodic assessments and provide recommendations for optimization.

Measure and communicate the business value of cyber investments. This can include metrics like reduced risk, improved efficiency, or enabled business opportunities. By demonstrating tangible returns, leaders can help ensure ongoing support and investment.

Effective long-term cyber budgeting requires a combination of strategic alignment, risk-based prioritization, flexibility, and continuous communication and optimization. By embedding these principles into the planning process, organizations can establish sustainable funding models that keep pace with the ever-changing cyber threat landscape.

Public-private partnerships

Public-private partnerships and industry collaboration are increasingly essential in the fight against cyber crime. No single organization can defend against all threats alone, and attackers often exploit the seams between different companies and sectors.

To balance competitive concerns with the benefits of collaboration, start by identifying trusted partners with shared interests and complementary capabilities. These may include industry peers, research institutions, law enforcement agencies, or government entities.

Establish clear guidelines and protocols for information sharing, including what data types will be shared, how it will be protected, and how it can be used. Consider using anonymized or aggregated data to protect sensitive details while enabling meaningful collaboration.

Participate in formal information sharing and analysis centers (ISACs) or organizations (ISAOs) for your sector. These provide structured mechanisms for sharing threat intelligence and best practices while maintaining appropriate safeguards.

Engage in joint training exercises or response planning with partners to build familiarity and trust before an incident occurs. Collaborate on research and development efforts to advance the state of the art in cyber.

Remember, cyber is not a zero-sum game. By working together to raise the bar for security across the ecosystem, organizations can create collective defense benefits that outweigh any individual competitive risks.

Strategic Alliances and Cyber Intelligence Sharing

Forming strategic alliances and sharing cyber intelligence is similar to the concept of a neighborhood watch but on a corporate level. Organizations can benefit from a collective early warning system that alerts them to emerging threats by collaborating with industry partners and sharing threat intelligence. Managed Security Service Providers (MSSPs) extend their expertise and resources, providing continuous support in implementing security solutions and monitoring threats. Additionally, engaging with government agencies can provide further insights into national cyber threats and best practices, serving as a valuable resource for up-to-date information.

Investing in the Future: R&D and Talent Development

Investing in cyber research and development (R&D) and talent development is similar to laying a solid foundation for your organization's digital security. Staying ahead of the curve through R&D helps businesses anticipate how emerging technologies like blockchain and quantum computing could impact security. This proactive stance helps in future-proofing against cyber criminals' evolving tactics. Moreover, the effectiveness of sophisticated security tools depends on the skills of the professionals who use them. Therefore, investing in cyber talent is critical. This could include sponsoring training programs, offering competitive compensation to attract top talent, or establishing internships to nurture future security experts. Encouraging continuous learning and awareness ensures that your security team remains knowledgeable about the latest threats and defense mechanisms.

Conclusion

Securing your organization's future in the digital age demands a proactive approach to cyber. By embracing technology, fostering a culture of security awareness, and building strategic partnerships, businesses can establish a strong defense against cyber threats. Remember, cyber is not a one-time effort but an ongoing process that requires constant adaptation and investment. The strategies outlined in this chapter can guide you in creating a future where your organization survives and thrives securely in the digital landscape.

Answers To Key Questions

Question 1: Ensuring an Agile and Responsive Cyber Strategy in a Rapidly Changing Landscape

Answer: The constant evolution of technology presents new challenges for cyber strategies. To maintain security, these strategies must be adaptable, responsive, and regularly reviewed for applicability. The key lies in anticipating threats. This can be achieved by monitoring geopolitical developments, threat intelligence feeds, and industry reports and actively participating in information-sharing communities. By staying informed, you can adjust your defenses before new threats become problematic.

Regular testing is crucial. Penetration testing and vulnerability assessments identify weaknesses in your security posture before attackers can exploit them. Security reviews at set intervals ensure that your existing strategies are effective and can be improved upon.

Flexibility is essential when it comes to security solutions. Consider cloud-based options that can quickly scale up or down to meet your needs. Finally, a strong learning culture within your security team is vital. Encourage them to attend conferences, workshops, and training programs to stay ahead of evolving attack techniques.

By prioritizing these practices, your cyber strategy will transform from a static shield into a dynamic one, capable of adapting and evolving alongside the ever-changing threat landscape.

Question 2: What key indicators signal the need to shift or upgrade our cyber approach?

Answer: The signs that your cyber needs attention are not always dramatic. Sometimes, it's a subtle shift, such as a gradual increase in near-misses with phishing emails or a piece of malware that a slightly outdated antivirus doesn't recognize. This uptick in incidents is a crucial indicator: your existing protections are being tested and might not withstand a more severe attack. Similarly, relying on older security technology leaves you vulnerable, as attackers constantly develop new ways to bypass yesterday's defenses.

Another telling sign is the difficulty in complying with regulations. Data security rules are continually changing, and if you find it increasingly challenging to meet industry or government standards, your technical safeguards and security practices likely need to be updated. Finally, look to your people as well: successful phishing attacks often emphasize the need for better training. Even well-intentioned employees can sometimes be the weakest link if they lack the awareness to spot social engineering tactics.

None of these signs indicate an immediate crisis, but they shouldn't be ignored. Recognizing these indicators allows you to bolster your defenses, upgrade tools, implement more robust training, and adapt your cyber strategies before vulnerabilities can be exploited.

Question 3: How can we effectively balance innovation and risk management in an increasingly digital and interconnected business landscape?

Answer: Now more than ever, Innovation is essential for staying competitive. However, prioritizing security alongside innovation is non-negotiable. The key is to make security an integral part of development. By considering cyber implications from the start of any project, you avoid vulnerabilities hindering progress further down the line. Remember, 'secure by design' is critical to your success.

Proactive risk assessment also plays a vital role. Before embarking on new initiatives, thoroughly analyze the potential risks to protect your systems and ensure delays due to security issues don't undermine your goals. Likewise, adopting a mindset of threat modeling, where you anticipate how attackers might target your new technologies, allows you to address potential weaknesses before they're exploited.

Finally, collaboration is paramount. Designate security champions within different teams to promote communication and understanding. This collaboration ensures that everyone, from developers and IT professionals to business leaders, is responsible for securing innovation.

Adopting these strategies creates a culture where robust security fuels innovation rather than hinders it. This allows your business to embrace new technologies and stay competitive confidently.

Question 4: What steps can we take to embed a proactive cyber mindset across all levels of the organization?

Answer: Creating a culture of cyber isn't just about technology – it's about people. Start with establishing a proactive governance structure that manages cyber risk throughout the organization. Comprehensive training beyond technical jargon, including simulations, role-playing, and games, keeps it engaging. Security awareness shouldn't be a once-a-year checkbox; make it a continuous process tailored to every employee's role. This can't succeed without strong leadership support. Executives have the power to set the tone. They should publicly champion security, tie it directly to business success, and participate visibly in awareness activities.

It's also essential to communicate consistently. Updates, incident reports (without compromising sensitive details), and lessons learned keep security at the forefront of everyone's minds. But this shouldn't be one-sided – empower your employees to speak up. Provide straightforward ways to report suspicious activity without fear so minor incidents are caught before they escalate. Finally, reward security-conscious behavior. Public recognition, awards, and even tying it to performance reviews demonstrate that security isn't just a chore; it's a core part of everyone's responsibilities.

By taking these steps, you move from merely defending against cyber attacks to a proactive stance. Your entire organization becomes a force multiplier, making it far more challenging for any threat actor to succeed.

Question 5: How can we ensure that cyber considerations are an integral part of our decision-making processes at the executive level?

Answer: Executives often focus on profits, market share, and innovation. Cyber can seem like an abstract technical concern, but it needs equal weight in the boardroom. This starts with translating security into business language. Frame risks in terms of lost revenue, damaged reputation, or how downtime might cripple operations – figures executives clearly understand. Every Board should have an executive charged with owning the cyber risk for the organization who is empowered to make decisions on behalf of the board if required, and this individual heads up the organization's cyber risk governance structure.

Alongside this, security impact assessments should be made routine for significant decisions. Experts should map the security risks before launching a new product or expanding into a new region. This doesn't block progress but allows executives to make those decisions with a complete understanding, balancing risk and reward.

It is vital to include security professionals in strategic discussions from the beginning. Their technical expertise identifies potential threats early, guiding decisions toward secure, innovative solutions rather than leaving security as a costly afterthought.

Finally, track and report key security metrics. Numbers like vulnerability patching speed, incident response times, and training completion rates demonstrate that security investment has tangible benefits. This continuous reporting reinforces that cyber is an ongoing core concern, not a one-off expense.

By embedding these practices into executive decision-making, security isn't seen as an obstacle but an enabler. This allows for bold business choices with the confidence that the organization's reputation and bottom line are protected.

Question 6: How can we encourage and facilitate cross-departmental collaboration to enhance our overall cyber posture?

Answer: Cyber can't exist in isolation. Breaking down silos between teams is crucial for any organization to create a strong defensive front. One critical step is defining roles clearly. Effective cyber is a leadership issue and should start with a board-level executive who is made responsible for ensuring cyber becomes a horizontal pillar cutting across all departments in an organization. It's one thing to task IT with security, but it's far more effective if other departments see their specific responsibilities: Marketing, educating customers, HR reinforcing secure practices, etc.

Alongside this, communication is vital. Regular cross-team meetings and dedicated collaboration platforms enable the sharing of intel, the discussion of incidents, and the coordination of efforts. This creates shared accountability and combats the idea that cyber is solely an IT concern.

Focus this collaboration on joint projects – remember, cyber is a team sport! A team of HR, IT, and Marketing personnel tackling phishing awareness is far more effective than each acting alone. These projects build bridges, foster a sense of shared goals, and produce tangible results.

Finally, track and reward successful collaboration. Publicly recognizing teams who work together to improve security reinforces its importance across the organization. When departments feel their collaboration is valued, they seek further opportunities to create a united front against cyber attacks. Lastly, spread and ensure best practices are adopted throughout the organization.

Question 7: How can strategic alliances and partnerships enhance our cyber intelligence and threat response capabilities?

Answer: The adage "two heads are better than one" applies just as strongly to cyber. Start with threat intelligence sharing. Joining forces with industry peers or specialized organizations gives you access to a broader pool of knowledge about emerging threats. This lets you anticipate and prepare defenses before those threats become your problem.

Joint exercises with partners also have significant value. Simulations test your response procedures far better than any theoretical discussion and allow you to learn from others' experiences handling similar incidents. Sometimes, collaboration can extend further. Working with security vendors or researchers can open the door to cutting-edge solutions tailored to your needs.

By thinking beyond your organization's borders and seeking out these strategic partnerships, you can access resources and knowledge that would not be possible alone. These alliances give you an edge in the constantly evolving fight against cyber threats, strengthening your ability to not just react to incidents but prevent them entirely.

Question 8: What are the best practices for sharing cyber intelligence while protecting sensitive company information?

Answer: Sharing threat intelligence is vital for staying ahead of attackers, but that doesn't mean giving away the keys to the kingdom. Start with clear, formal agreements. These define what data can be shared, how detailed it can be, and the specific security protocols that must be followed. This ensures everyone understands the rules, protecting privacy on both sides.

Consider anonymizing data whenever possible. Removing names and specific system details – anything that ties an incident too closely to your organization – lets you contribute helpful information without jeopardizing confidentiality. Also, pay close attention to the technical side: strong passwords, multi-factor authentication, and encryption for all shared data are absolute must-haves.

Finally, the power of intelligence sharing truly emerges during a crisis. Pre-established plans for coordinating incident response with trusted partners create a unified front. This makes you all more resilient, minimizing the damage any one organization might suffer.

Following these practices builds strong, secure bridges within the security community. This allows for crucial information sharing while keeping your sensitive data safe.

Question 9: How do we evaluate and choose the right partners for cyber collaboration that align with our business values and security needs?

Answer: Choosing a cyber partner is like adding a key member to your team – you need a good fit. Start by looking at their security philosophy. Are their practices rigorous? Do they handle data responsibly? Public-facing certifications and a clean track record in handling incidents are good signs. Finding a partner who shares your stance on security creates a foundation of trust.

Next, consider what they bring to the table. Do their skills complement yours? A specialist security firm might offer expertise your internal IT lacks, while a research-focused partner might give you access to cutting-edge threat intelligence.

Think about the long term as well: Are they scalable? Can they grow alongside your business and meet new needs as they emerge? Security challenges are dynamic, and you need a partner capable of adapting.

Finally, don't overlook the human aspect. Can your team work with them? Open communication is crucial, but it has to feel natural. Do your technical staff feel comfortable raising issues and engaging their expertise? Mutual respect and ease of communication are essential for productive collaboration.

By considering these factors, you're more likely to select a cyber partner who will be a true asset, align with your values, strengthen your defenses, and evolve alongside your organization as it faces future security challenges.

Question 10: How should we approach investments in cyber R&D to ensure they are forward-thinking and yield tangible benefits?

Answer: Cyber R&D isn't about fixing today's problems but preventing tomorrow's issues. Start by focusing on where technology is heading: Artificial intelligence, expanded cloud use, and the ever-growing Internet of Things have significant security implications. Proactive research in these areas allows you to anticipate threats and get ahead of them.

Universities and specialized research firms are often at the forefront of security innovation. Partnering with these institutions grants access to their expertise and can guide your investments into areas with the most significant potential impact. Remember to nurture innovation at home, however. Providing time and resources for your team to explore new ideas can uncover surprising solutions. Hackathons, research competitions, and focused training all foster this spirit of discovery.

Finally, remember that R&D needs to have a measurable payoff. Tracking vulnerabilities found, solutions developed, and the cost of attacks prevented justifies continued investment. By making the business case for forward-thinking security research, you ensure your organization won't just survive the next wave of attacks—it will thrive knowing it's prepared for whatever comes after.

Question 11: What strategies can we employ to attract, retain, and develop top talent in the cyber field within our organization?

Answer: Finding great cyber professionals is only half the battle – you must convince them to stay. Start, of course, with competitive pay and benefits. Don't just meet industry standards; aim to exceed them and ensure your benefits show an understanding of cyber workers' specific needs. But money isn't everything. Cyber is a high-pressure field. A healthy work culture is vital. Celebrate teamwork, encourage open communication, and actively work to prevent burnout.

Alongside this, show them a path forward in your organization. Generous support for certifications and training signals you're invested in their growth, and internal mentorship programs create bonds within the team. Finally, highlight the impactful nature of the work itself. Cyber is never dull! Showcase their exciting challenges and consider bug bounty programs where they can flex their skills outside of day-to-day tasks.

By creating a workplace where security pros are well-compensated, feel cared for, and are continuously challenged, you're not just hiring staff – you're building a team with loyalty and drive that's hard for any competitor to match.

Question 12: How can we measure the effectiveness and impact of our cyber talent and R&D investments on our overall security posture and business success?

Answer: Spending money on cyber is easy, but proving it's worth it is more challenging. Start with the obvious metrics – fewer vulnerabilities found, faster response times, and a decline in successful attacks – these show your defenses are getting stronger. Track them consistently to show trends, not just single data points.

But it's not just about stopping attacks. Think about the cost of failure: lost data, reputation damage, and the business grinding to a halt. Compare these potential losses to your security spending to illustrate the return on investment. Effective cyber can also improve your business in surprising ways. Streamlining security processes can free your IT staff to work on other crucial tasks. Likewise, reduced downtime due to robust security is an efficiency win with a tangible business payoff.

By quantifying these benefits, you move beyond just asking for a security budget. You make a powerful argument that cyber investment isn't just a cost but a driver of efficiency and a safeguard against potentially ruinous losses. This ensures that the resources needed for solid security are never considered optional.

Further Reading

1. Rothrock, R. (2020). Digital resilience: Is your company ready for the next cyberthreat? AMACOM.

2. Johansen, B. (2017). The new leadership literacies: Thriving in a future of extreme disruption and distributed everything.

Berrett-Koehler Publishers.

3. Senge, P. M. (2006). The fifth discipline: The art & practice of the learning organization. Crown Business.

4. National Institute of Standards and Technology. (2020). NIST special publication 800-160, volume 2: Developing cyberresilient systems: A systems security engineering approach. https://doi.org/10.6028/NIST.SP.800-160v2

5. World Economic Forum. (2020). The global risks report 2020. https://www.weforum.org/reports/the-global-risks-report-2020

Conclusion

Embracing Cyber Security is a Leadership Imperative

Throughout this book, we have explored the critical importance of cyber security in the modern business landscape. From understanding the evolving threat landscape and applying effective risk management strategies to fostering a culture of security awareness and investing wisely in defensive measures, we have provided a comprehensive guide for leaders to navigate the complexities of the digital world.

The key takeaway is clear: cyber security is no longer an optional consideration but an absolute necessity for any organization that hopes to thrive in the face of relentless digital threats. As technology advances at an unprecedented pace, the potential attack surface expands, and cyber criminals' sophistication grows. In this environment, a proactive, adaptable, and deeply integrated approach to cyber security is not just a best practice but a business imperative.

This imperative starts with a fundamental shift in mindset. Cyber security can no longer be relegated to the IT department or treated as an afterthought. It must be recognized as a strategic priority deeply intertwined with every aspect of the business, from product development and customer service to financial planning and risk management. Leaders at every level, from the boardroom to the front lines, must understand their critical role in protecting the organization's digital assets and reputation.

This shift in mindset must be accompanied by concrete action. Organizations must invest in robust technical defenses, including firewalls, intrusion detection systems, and encryption tools. They must implement stringent access controls and data management policies to minimize the risk of insider threats. They must work tirelessly to identify and patch vulnerabilities before attackers can exploit them.

But technology alone is not enough. The human element is just as critical. Every employee, from the CEO to the newest hire, must be trained and empowered to serve as a line of defense against cyber threats. Regular security awareness training and a culture that encourages vigilance and rewards secure behavior can transform the workforce into a powerful ally in the fight against cyber crime.

Leaders must also recognize that cyber security is not a one-time project but an ongoing process of continuous improvement. The threat landscape constantly evolves, and organizations must be agile enough to adapt their defenses in real-time. This requires robust threat intelligence capabilities, close collaboration with industry partners and government agencies, and a willingness to learn from every incident, whether successful or thwarted.

Equally important is the need for cyber resilience. No defense is perfect; even the most secure organizations can fall victim to a well-crafted attack. The ability to detect, respond to, and recover from incidents quickly and effectively is just as crucial as preventing them in the first place. A comprehensive incident response plan, regularly tested and updated, can mean the difference between a minor disruption and a catastrophic breach.

The benefits of a robust cyber security posture extend far beyond risk mitigation. In an era where "data is the new oil", customers, partners, and investors increasingly base their trust and loyalty on an organization's ability to protect their sensitive information. A reputation for security excellence can be a powerful competitive differentiator, opening doors to new markets and opportunities. Conversely, a single high-profile breach can inflict lasting damage on a company's brand and bottom line.

For business leaders, the message is clear. Embracing the cyber security imperative is not just about defending against threats but also enabling the organization to innovate, grow, and thrive in the digital age. By strategically investing in people, processes, and technology, fostering a culture of shared responsibility and continuous learning, and remaining ever vigilant in the face of evolving dangers, leaders can position their organizations for success in a world where cyber security is no longer optional but essential.

What Next

The path forward is not always easy, but it is necessary. The stakes are too high, and the threats are too significant to ignore. But with the right mindset, strategies, and partners, any organization can rise to the challenge and secure its place in the digital future.

We hope this book has provided you with the knowledge, insights, and tools you need to lead your organization on this critical journey. By embracing the cyber security imperative, you are not just protecting your company's assets and reputation but building a foundation for long-term success and resilience in an increasingly connected and challenging world.

The time to act is now. The threat is real, but so is the opportunity. By taking the lessons of this book to heart and putting them into practice, you can position your organization at the forefront of the cyber security revolution and help shape a safer, more prosperous digital future for all.

Lastly, we wanted to thank you for buying the book and taking the time to read it. If you have found this useful we would be very grateful if you would leave us a review (see opposite). There are other books in the "Leadership Impact Series," and we would encourage you to explore these as well.

Marco and Andrew

London, May 2024

Chapter 13

About The Authors

Marco Ryan

Marco is a renowned expert in digital transformation, data management, Artificial Intelligence, and Cyber. With a comprehensive understanding of the evolving digital landscape, gained through years of Operational experience Marco brings a wealth of experience and expertise to guide readers through the world of Artificial Intelligence, Cyber and Digital Transformation.

As the Cyber Leader in Residence at Lancaster University Management School and a former Global Chief Digital Officer and Senior Vice President Digital for BP, Marco is committed to empowering readers with the knowledge and skills necessary to navigate the digital future.

He has extensive public speaking experience, including Ted talks, regularly delivering keynotes at major conferences or for companies as part of workshops or off-sites.

To discuss options for working with Marco, whether for group or individual coaching or to explore having him deliver a keynote address, please use the QR code or click the link to his website.

https://marcoryan.com

Andrew Fitzmaurice

Andrew is CEO of Templar Executives, an international, award winning cyber advisory company; he leads an expert management team delivering world-class cyber consultancy services and solutions. Andrew specialises in government and commercial sector board-level engagements and transformational change programmes to enhance business performance. He has also established the Templar Cyber Academy whose range of courses and training are uniquely certified by the National Cyber Security Centre (NCSC).

Lancaster University

A thought leader and accomplished speaker and author, Andrew is regularly invited to contribute and speak on Cyber, Information Assurance and Governance topics. He, in partnership with Lancaster University, has led the development of a Cyber Executive MBA aimed at senior executives. He is strategic advisor to the Global Capacity Building Centre at the Oxford Martin School at Oxford University. He has also taken part in the FCO Commonwealth Cyber Security Programme as a mentor to Ministers from the Commonwealth Countries.

Andrew's background includes 18 years in the military specialising in air command and control. He has worked in the Cabinet Office where he set up and ran the Office of the Government Senior Information Risk Owner (OGSIRO). Andrew has also been closely involved in authoring key publications and policies including: The Data Handling Review (Hannigan Report); The IA Diagnostic Methodology; the Ministry of Defence Information Assurance Strategy and the UK's National Information Assurance/Cyber strategies.

https://templarexecs.com

Book Review Request

"If your actions inspire others to dream more, learn more, do more and become more, you are a leader."
~ John Quincy Adams

We hope that you are finding the book useful. I suspect that there are many other leaders out there, who were like you used to be. Less experienced, needing answers, but not sure who or what to trust.

Most people do, in fact, judge a book by its cover (and its reviews). So here's my request to you as an amazing leader who I know is committed to helping others succeed.

Please help that leader by leaving this book a review.

It's remarkably hassle-free, it doesn't cost you anything, it will take about 60 seconds and your review really could help.

If you are on audible - hit the three dots in the top right of your device, click rate & review, then leave a few sentences about the book with a star rating.

If you are reading on kindle, iPad or other tablet - scroll to the bottom of the book, then swipe up and it will prompt a review for you.

If for some reason these are not working for you, then go to Amazon and leave a review right on the book's page. Here's the link: https://geni.us/review-101CyberAnswers

If all fails, scan this QR code:

Thank you for doing that. It makes more of a difference to the next leader who may be considering whether to get this book than you realize.

Please do also explore some of the other books in the "Leadership Impact Series" - we shall continue to add new titles through out the year.

Thank you so much

Marco and Andrew

London, May 2024

Resources

Chapter 1: Unveiling Digital Threat Vectors

Bendovschi, A. (2015). Cyber-attacks–trends, patterns and security countermeasures. Procedia Economics and Finance, 28, 24-31. https://doi.org/10.1016/S2212-5671(15)01077-1

Cisco. (2023). Cisco Annual Internet Report (2018–2023) White Paper. https://www.cisco.com/c/en/us/solutions/collateral/executive-perspectives/annual-internet-report/white-paper-c11-741490.html

Cybersecurity & Infrastructure Security Agency (CISA). (2020). Ransomware Guide. https://www.cisa.gov/publication/ransomware-guide

European Union Agency for Cybersecurity (ENISA). (2020). ENISA Threat Landscape 2020 - Botnet. https://www.enisa.

europa.eu/publications/enisa-threat-landscape-2020-botnet

Fruhlinger, J. (2020). The 15 biggest data breaches of the 21st century. CSO Online. https://www.csoonline.com/article/2130877/the-biggest-data-breaches-of-the-21st-century.html

Kaplan, J., Sharma, S., & Weinberg, A. (2011). Meeting the cybersecurity challenge. McKinsey Quarterly.

Lee, R. M., Assante, M. J., & Conway, T. (2016). Analysis of the cyber attack on the Ukrainian power grid. SANS Industrial Control Systems.

Osborne, C. (2021). The top 10 security incidents of 2021. ZDNet. https://www.zdnet.com/article/the-top-10-security-incidents-of-2021/

Tariq, M. I., Tayyaba, S., Rasheed, H., & Ashraf, M. W. (2017, March). Factors influencing the cloud computing adoption in higher education institutions of Punjab, Pakistan. In 2017 International Conference on Communication Technologies (ComTech) (pp. 44-49). IEEE.

Verizon. (2023). 2023 Data Breach Investigations Report. https://www.verizon.com/business/resources/reports/dbir/

Chapter 2: Applying Digital Risk Management For Business Optimization

Da Veiga, A., & Martins, N. (2015). Information security culture and information protection culture: A validated assessment instrument. Computer Law & Security Review, 31(2), 243-256. https://doi.org/10.1016/j.clsr.2015.01.005

Ernst & Young. (2020). Global Information Security Survey 2020. https://assets.ey.com/content/dam/ey-sites/ey-com/en_gl/

topics/advisory/ey-global-information-security-survey-2020-report-single-pages.pdf

Gartner. (2020). Gartner Forecasts Worldwide Security and Risk Management Spending Growth to Slow but Remain Positive in 2020. https://www.gartner.com/en/newsroom/press-releases/2020-06-17-gartner-forecasts-worldwide-security-and-risk-managem

Herath, T., & Rao, H. R. (2009). Protection motivation and deterrence: a framework for security policy compliance in organisations. European Journal of Information Systems, 18(2), 106-125. https://doi.org/10.1057/ejis.2009.6

Humphreys, E. (2008). Information security management standards: Compliance, governance and risk management. information security technical report, 13(4), 247-255. https://doi.org/10.1016/j.istr.2008.10.010

International Organization for Standardization (ISO). (2018). ISO 31000:2018 Risk management — Guidelines. https://www.iso.org/standard/65694.html

National Institute of Standards and Technology (NIST). (2018). Framework for improving critical infrastructure cybersecurity. https://doi.org/10.6028/NIST.CSWP.04162018

Ponemon Institute. (2020). Cost of a Data Breach Report 2020. https://www.ibm.com/security/digital-assets/cost-data-breach-report/

PwC. (2022). Global Digital Trust Insights 2022. https://www.pwc.com/us/en/services/consulting/cybersecurity-risk-regulatory/library/global-digital-trust-insights.html

Verizon. (2022). 2022 Data Breach Investigations Report. https://

www.verizon.com/business/resources/reports/dbir/

Chapter 3: Creating A Cyber Strategy Roadmap For Business

Bada, M., Sasse, A. M., & Nurse, J. R. (2019). Cyber security awareness campaigns: Why do they fail to change behaviour?. arXiv preprint arXiv:1901.02672.

Bartnes, M., Moe, N. B., & Heegaard, P. E. (2016). The future of information security incident management training: A case study of electrical power companies. Computers & Security, 61, 32-45. https://doi.org/10.1016/j.cose.2016.05.004

Boehm, B., & Turner, R. (2005). Management challenges to implementing agile processes in traditional development organizations. IEEE software, 22(5), 30-39. https://doi.org/10.1109/MS.2005.129

Center for Internet Security (CIS). (2019). The CIS Controls. https://www.cisecurity.org/controls/

Horne, C. A., Ahmad, A., & Maynard, S. B. (2016). A theory on information security. In Proceedings of the 27th Australasian Conference on Information Systems.

ISACA. (2019). COBIT 2019 Framework: Introduction and Methodology. https://www.isaca.org/bookstore/bookstore-cobit_19-digital/wcb19fmm

National Institute of Standards and Technology (NIST). (2020). Special Publication 800-53, Revision 5: Security and Privacy Controls for Information Systems and Organizations. https://doi.org/10.6028/NIST.SP.800-53r5

Nicho, M. (2018). A process model for implementing information systems security governance. Information & Computer Security. https://doi.org/10.1108/ICS-07-2016-0061

Schinagl, S., & Shahim, A. (2020). What do we know about information security governance? From the basement to the boardroom: towards digital security governance. Information & Computer Security, 28(2), 261-292. https://doi.org/10.1108/ICS-02-2019-0029

Von Solms, R., & Van Niekerk, J. (2013). From information security to cyber security. computers & security, 38, 97-102. https://doi.org/10.1016/j.cose.2013.04.004

Chapter 4: Understanding The Complexity Of Cyber Law And Ethics

Chertoff, M. (2018). Exploding Data: Reclaiming Our Cyber Security in the Digital Age. Atlantic Monthly Press.

Deibert, R. J. (2013). Black code: Inside the battle for cyberspace. Signal/McClelland & Stewart.

International Telecommunication Union (ITU). (2021). Global Cybersecurity Index 2020. https://www.itu.int/en/ITU-D/Cybersecurity/Pages/global-cybersecurity-index.aspx

Jarvis, L., & Macdonald, S. (2015). What is cyberterrorism? Findings from a survey of researchers. Terrorism and Political Violence, 27(4), 657-678. https://doi.org/10.1080/09546553.2013.847827

Lessig, L. (2006). Code: Version 2.0. Basic Books.

Lin, P., Abney, K., & Bekey, G. A. (Eds.). (2011). Robot ethics: The ethical and social implications of robotics. MIT Press.

Moore, A. D. (2010). Privacy rights: Moral and legal foundations. Penn State Press.

Nissenbaum, H. (2009). Privacy in context: Technology, policy, and the integrity of social life. Stanford University Press.

Solove, D. J. (2008). Understanding privacy (Vol. 10). Harvard University Press.

Weber, R. H., & Weber, R. (2010). Internet of things: Legal perspectives (Vol. 49). Springer Science & Business Media.

Chapter 5: Leading Cyber Culture From The C-Suite

Barton, K. A., Tejay, G., Lane, M., & Terrell, S. (2016). Information system security commitment: A study of external influences on senior management. Computers & Security, 59, 9-25. https://doi.org/10.1016/j.cose.2016.02.007

Da Veiga, A. (2016). Comparing the information security culture of employees who had read the information security policy and those who had not. Information & Computer Security. https://doi.org/10.1108/ICS-12-2015-0048

Herath, T., & Rao, H. R. (2009). Encouraging information security behaviors in organizations: Role of penalties, pressures and perceived effectiveness. Decision Support Systems, 47(2), 154-165. https://doi.org/10.1016/j.dss.2009.02.005

Hu, Q., Dinev, T., Hart, P., & Cooke, D. (2012). Managing employee compliance with information security policies: The critical role of top management and organizational culture. Decision Sciences,

43(4), 615-660. https://doi.org/10.1111/j.1540-5915.2012.00361.x

Knapp, K. J., Marshall, T. E., Rainer, R. K., & Ford, F. N. (2006). Information security: management's effect on culture and policy. Information Management & Computer Security. https://doi.org/10.1108/09685220610648355

Martins, A., & Elofe, J. (2002). Information security culture. In Security in the information society (pp. 203-214). Springer, Boston, MA. https://doi.org/10.1007/978-0-387-35586-3_16

Roer, K. (2015). Build a security culture. IT Governance Ltd.

Soomro, Z. A., Shah, M. H., & Ahmed, J. (2016). Information security management needs more holistic approach: A literature review. International Journal of Information Management, 36(2), 215-225. https://doi.org/10.1016/j.ijinfomgt.2015.11.009

Van Niekerk, J. F., & Von Solms, R. (2010). Information security culture: A management perspective. Computers & Security, 29(4), 476-486. https://doi.org/10.1016/j.cose.2009.10.005

Von Solms, B., & Von Solms, R. (2018). Cybersecurity and information security–what goes where?. Information & Computer Security. https://doi.org/10.1108/ICS-04-2017-0025

Dimon, J. (2021). CEO Letter to Shareholders. JPMorgan Chase & Co. https://reports.jpmorganchase.com/investor-relations/2020/ar-ceo-letters.htm

Huston, P. (2020, November). Why every CEO should join the 'Hacker in Chief' club. World Economic Forum. https://www.weforum.org/agenda/2020/11/ceo-hacker-in-chief-club-cybersecurity/

IBM. (2021). Security Education and Training. https://www.ibm.

com/security/services/security-education-and-training

Lockheed Martin. (2021). Cybersecurity. https://www.lockheedmartin.com/en-us/capabilities/cyber.html

Microsoft. (2021). Digital Diplomacy: Strengthening international cybersecurity. https://www.microsoft.com/en-us/cybersecurity/digital-diplomacy

National Institute of Standards and Technology (NIST). (2021). Cybersecurity Framework. https://www.nist.gov/cyberframework

Siemens. (2021). Cyber Heroes: Empowering our employees to strengthen cybersecurity. https://new.siemens.com/global/en/company/stories/research-technologies/cybersecurity/cyber-heroes.html

U.S. Department of Justice. (2021). Former Coca-Cola Employee Sentenced for Stealing Trade Secrets. https://www.justice.gov/usao-ndga/pr/former-coca-cola-employee-sentenced-stealing-trade-secrets

Chapter 6: Cyber As An Investment, Not An Expense

Baskerville, R., Spagnoletti, P., & Kim, J. (2014). Incident-centered information security: Managing a strategic balance between prevention and response. Information & Management, 51(1), 138-151. https://doi.org/10.1016/j.im.2013.11.004

Bodin, L. D., Gordon, L. A., & Loeb, M. P. (2005). Evaluating information security investments using the analytic hierarchy process. Communications of the ACM, 48(2), 78-83. https://doi.

org/10.1145/1042091.1042094

Böhme, R., & Nowey, T. (2008, October). Economic security metrics. In Dependability metrics (pp. 176-187). Springer, Berlin, Heidelberg. https://doi.org/10.1007/978-3-540-68947-8_15

Demetz, L., & Bachlechner, D. (2013). To invest or not to invest? Assessing the economic viability of a policy and security configuration management tool. In The economics of information security and privacy (pp. 25-47). Springer, Berlin, Heidelberg. https://doi.org/10.1007/978-3-642-39498-0_2

Gordon, L. A., & Loeb, M. P. (2002). The economics of information security investment. ACM Transactions on Information and System Security (TISSEC), 5(4), 438-457. https://doi.org/10.1145/581271.581274

Gordon, L. A., Loeb, M. P., & Sohail, T. (2010). Market value of voluntary disclosures concerning information security. MIS quarterly, 567-594. https://doi.org/10.2307/25750692

Hoo, K. J. S. (2000). How much is enough? A risk management approach to computer security.

Huang, C. D., Hu, Q., & Behara, R. S. (2008). An economic analysis of the optimal information security investment in the case of a risk-averse firm. International Journal of Production Economics, 114(2), 793-804. https://doi.org/10.1016/j.ijpe.2008.04.002

Purser, S. A. (2004). Improving the ROI of the security management process. Computers & Security, 23(7), 542-546. https://doi.org/10.1016/j.cose.2004.09.004

Rue, R., Pfleeger, S. L., & Ortiz, D. (2007). A framework for classifying and comparing models of cyber security investment to support policy and decision-making. In Proceedings of the sixth annual workshop on the economics of information security.

Chapter 7: Cultivating Cyber Guardians: Building a Human Firewall

Albrechtsen, E., & Hovden, J. (2010). Improving information security awareness and behaviour through dialogue, participation and collective reflection. An intervention study. Computers & Security, 29(4), 432-445. https://doi.org/10.1016/j.cose.2009.12.005

Bauer, S., Bernroider, E. W., & Chudzikowski, K. (2017). Prevention is better than cure! Designing information security awareness programs to overcome users' non-compliance with information security policies in banks. Computers & Security, 68, 145-159. https://doi.org/10.1016/j.cose.2017.04.009

Bada, M., Sasse, A. M., & Nurse, J. R. (2019). Cyber security awareness campaigns: Why do they fail to change behaviour?. arXiv preprint arXiv:1901.02672.

Dodge Jr, R. C., Carver, C., & Ferguson, A. J. (2007). Phishing for user security awareness. computers & security, 26(1), 73-80. https://doi.org/10.1016/j.cose.2006.10.009

Henshel, D., Cains, M. G., Hoffman, B., & Kelley, T. (2015). Trust as a human factor in holistic cybersecurity risk assessment. Procedia Manufacturing, 3, 1117-1124. https://doi.org/10.1016/j.promfg.2015.07.186

Lebek, B., Uffen, J., Neumann, M., Hohler, B., & H. Breitner, M. (2014). Information security awareness and behavior: a theory-based literature review. Management Research Review

McCormac, A., Zwaans, T., Parsons, K., Calic, D., Butavicius, M., & Pattinson, M. (2017). Individual differences and information security awareness. Computers in Human Behavior, 69, 151-156. https://doi.org/10.1016/j.chb.2016.11.065

Öğütçü, G., Testik, Ö. M., & Chouseinoglou, O. (2016). Analysis of personal information security behavior and awareness. Computers & Security, 56, 83-93. https://doi.org/10.1016/j.cose.2015.10.002

Parsons, K., McCormac, A., Butavicius, M., Pattinson, M., & Jerram, C. (2014). Determining employee awareness using the Human Aspects of Information Security Questionnaire (HAIS-Q). Computers & Security, 42, 165-176. https://doi.org/10.1016/j.cose.2013.12.003

Puhakainen, P., & Siponen, M. (2010). Improving employees' compliance through information systems security training: an action research study. MIS quarterly, 757-778. https://doi.org/10.2307/25750704

Chapter 8: Securing The Supply Chain Ecosystem

Boyens, J., Paulsen, C., Moorthy, R., & Bartol, N. (2015). Supply chain risk management practices for federal information systems and organizations. NIST Special Publication, 800(161), 1-282. https://doi.org/10.6028/NIST.SP.800-161

Durowoju, O. A., Chan, H. K., & Wang, X. (2011). Entropy assessment of supply chain disruption. Journal of Manufacturing Technology Management. https://doi.org/10.1108/17410381111126427

Gasper, P. (2021). The state of supply chain security and trust. PwC.

Ho, W., Zheng, T., Yildiz, H., & Talluri, S. (2015). Supply chain risk management: a literature review. International Journal of

Production Research, 53(16), 5031-5069. https://doi.org/10.1080/00207543.2015.1030467

Johnson, G. J. (2021). AI automation can mitigate impacts of supply chain disruptions and cybersecurity risks. Journal of Business Continuity & Emergency Planning, 15(2), 138-143.

Manges, K., & Scott-Cawiezell, J. (2021). Supply chain security through blockchain technology: a systematic review. Journal of medical systems, 45(12), 1-12. https://doi.org/10.1007/s10916-021-01789-6

Nogueira, V., Di Francesco Maesa, D., Menezes, A., & Martinelli, R. (2019, May). Cybersecurity challenges in the Industry 4.0 era. In Proceedings of the 14th International Symposium on Software Engineering for Adaptive and Self-Managing Systems (pp. 49-52). IEEE. https://doi.org/10.1109/SEAMS.2019.00016

Pandey, S. K., Srivastava, S., & Mishra, V. (2021). An integrated framework for supply chain risk management: A review. IOP Conference Series: Materials Science and Engineering, 1131(1), 012016. https://doi.org/10.1088/1757-899X/1131/1/012016

Ranise, S., & Viganò, L. (2021). Security Certification in the EU: The EU Cybersecurity Act and the Challenges Ahead. IEEE Security & Privacy, 19(3), 19-27. https://doi.org/10.1109/MSEC.2021.3058907

Yoon, J., Talluri, S., Yildiz, H., & Ho, W. (2018). Models for supplier selection and risk mitigation: A holistic approach. International Journal of Production Research, 56(10), 3636-3661. https://doi.or

g/10.1080/00207543.2017.1403662

Chapter 9: Proactive Cyber Incident Management

Ahmad, A., Maynard, S. B., & Park, S. (2014). Information security strategies: towards an organizational multi-strategy perspective. Journal of Intelligent Manufacturing, 25(2), 357-370. https://doi.org/10.1007/s10845-012-0683-0

Cichonski, P., Millar, T., Grance, T., & Scarfone, K. (2012). Computer security incident handling guide (No. Special Publication (NIST SP)-800-61r2).

Grispos, G., Glisson, W. B., & Storer, T. (2015, January). Security incident response criteria: A practitioner's perspective. In 2015 Americas Conference on Information Systems, AMCIS 2015. Association for Information Systems.

Killcrece, G., Kossakowski, K. P., Ruefle, R., & Zajicek, M. (2003). State of the practice of computer security incident response teams (CSIRTs) (No. CMU/SEI-2003-TR-001). Carnegie-Mellon Univ Pittsburgh Pa Software Engineering Inst.

Mateski, M., Trevino, C. M., Veitch, C. K., Michalski, J., Harris, J. M., Maruoka, S., & Frye, J. (2012). Cyber threat metrics (No. SAND2012-2427). Sandia National Laboratories.

Mitropoulos, S., Patsos, D., & Douligeris, C. (2006). On incident handling and response: A state-of-the-art approach. Computers & Security, 25(5), 351-370. https://doi.org/10.1016/j.cose.2005.09.006

Northcutt, S. (2003). Computer Security Incident Handling: Step by Step, Version 2.3. 1. SANS Institute.

Ruefle, R., van Wyk, K., & Tosic, L. (2013). New Zealand security incident management guide for computer security incident response teams (CSIRTs). Centre for Critical Infrastructure Protection, Government Communications Security Bureau.

Tøndel, I. A., Line, M. B., & Jaatun, M. G. (2014). Information security incident management: Current practice as reported in the literature. Computers & Security, 45, 42-57. https://doi.org/10.1016/j.cose.2014.05.003

Werlinger, R., Muldner, K., Hawkey, K., & Beznosov, K. (2010). Preparation, detection, and analysis: the diagnostic work of IT security incident response. Information Management & Computer Security.

Chapter 10: Picking The Right Cyber Defense Tools

Farris, K. A., Shah, A., Cybenko, G., Ganesan, R., & Jajodia, S. (2018). Vulcon: A system for vulnerability prioritization, conservation, and mitigation. In Proceedings of the 2018 ACM SIGSAC Conference on Computer and Communications Security (pp. 1049-1061). https://doi.org/10.1145/3243734.3243738

Kotenko, I., & Chechulin, A. (2013). A cyber attack modeling and impact assessment framework. In 2013 5th international conference on cyber conflict (CYCON 2013) (pp. 1-24). IEEE.

Llansó, T., McNeil, M., & Noteboom, C. (2019). Multi-criteria selection of capability-based cybersecurity solutions. In Proceedings of the 52nd Hawaii International Conference on System Sciences. http://hdl.handle.net/10125/60137

Ou, X., Boyer, W. F., & McQueen, M. A. (2006, December). A

scalable approach to attack graph generation. In Proceedings of the 13th ACM conference on Computer and communications security (pp. 336-345). https://doi.org/10.1145/1180405.1180446

Romanosky, S., Telang, R., & Acquisti, A. (2011). Do data breach disclosure laws reduce identity theft?. Journal of Policy Analysis and Management, 30(2), 256-286. https://doi.org/10.1002/pam.20567

Shah, A., Ganesan, R., Jajodia, S., & Cam, H. (2018). Understanding tradeoffs between throughput, quality, and cost of alert analysis in a csoc. IEEE Transactions on Information Forensics and Security, 14(5), 1155-1170. https://doi.org/10.1109/TIFS.2018.2878827

Sawik, T. (2013). Selection of optimal countermeasure portfolio in IT security planning. Decision Support Systems, 55(1), 156-164. https://doi.org/10.1016/j.dss.2013.01.001

Scarfone, K., & Mell, P. (2007). Guide to intrusion detection and prevention systems (idps) (No. Special Publication (NIST SP)-800-94). National Institute of Standards and Technology.

Sun, L., Srivastava, R. P., & Mock, T. J. (2006). An information systems security risk assessment model under the Dempster-Shafer theory of belief functions. Journal of Management Information Systems, 22(4), 109-142. https://doi.org/10.2753/MIS0742-1222220405

Viduto, V., Maple, C., Huang, W., & López-Peréz, D. (2012). A novel risk assessment and optimisation model for a multi-objective network security countermeasure selection problem. Decision Support Systems, 53(3), 599-610. https://doi.org/10.1016/j.

dss.2012.03.001

Chapter 11: Secure Innovation As A Competitive Advantage

Bulgurcu, B., Cavusoglu, H., & Benbasat, I. (2010). Information security policy compliance: an empirical study of rationality-based beliefs and information security awareness. MIS quarterly, 523-548. https://doi.org/10.2307/25750690

Cárdenas, A. A., Manadhata, P. K., & Rajan, S. P. (2013). Big data analytics for security. IEEE Security & Privacy, 11(6), 74-76. https://doi.org/10.1109/MSP.2013.138

Cavusoglu, H., Cavusoglu, H., & Raghunathan, S. (2004). Economics of IT security management: Four improvements to current security practices. The Communications of the Association for Information Systems, 14(1), 65. https://doi.org/10.17705/1CAIS.01403

Clarke, R. A., & Knake, R. K. (2014). Cyber war. Tantor Media, Incorporated.

Ekelhart, A., Fenz, S., Klemen, M. D., & Weippl, E. R. (2007, October). Security ontology: Simulating threats to corporate assets. In International Conference on Information Systems Security (pp. 249-259). Springer, Berlin, Heidelberg. https://doi.org/10.1007/978-3-540-77086-2_21

Kaplan, J., Sharma, S., & Weinberg, A. (2011). Meeting the cybersecurity challenge. McKinsey Quarterly.

PWC (2021) Global Digital Trust Insights Survey 2021

Ramamurthy, B. (2020). Principles of secure network systems

design. Springer Nature.

Soomro, Z. A., Shah, M. H., & Ahmed, J. (2016). Information security management needs more holistic approach: A literature review. International Journal of Information Management, 36(2), 215-225. https://doi.org/10.1016/j.ijinfomgt.2015.11.009

Xie, P., Li, J. H., Ou, X., Liu, P., & Levy, R. (2010, June). Using Bayesian networks for cyber security analysis. In 2010 IEEE/IFIP International Conference on Dependable Systems & Networks (DSN) (pp. 211-220). IEEE. https://doi.org/10.1109/DSN.2010.5544924

Chapter 12: Shaping Your Future Cyber Success

Al-Mohannadi, H., Mirza, Q., Namanya, A., Awan, I., Cullen, A., & Disso, J. (2016, April). Cyber-attack modeling analysis techniques: An overview. In 2016 IEEE 4th international conference on future internet of things and cloud workshops (FiCloudW) (pp. 69-76). IEEE. https://doi.org/10.1109/W-FiCloud.2016.29

Antonucci, D. (2017). The cyber risk handbook: Creating and measuring effective cybersecurity capabilities. John Wiley & Sons.

Bronfman, S. V., & Moskowitz, S. L. (2021). The future of cybersecurity: Major role of artificial intelligence, machine learning, and deep learning in cyberspace. In Artificial intelligence for future generation robotics (pp. 377-393). Academic Press. https://doi.org/10.1016/B978-0-12-823866-4.00019-5

Caldwell, T. (2013). Plugging the cyber-security skills gap. Computer Fraud & Security, 2013(7), 5-10. https://doi.

org/10.1016/S1361-3723(13)70062-9

Djenna, A., & Harous, S. (2021). Survey on the use of artificial intelligence for cyber security. In 2021 12th International Conference on Information and Communication Systems (ICICS) (pp. 47-52). IEEE. https://doi.org/10.1109/ICICS52457.2021.9464550

Haren, P., & Simchi-Levi, D. (2020). How coronavirus could impact the global supply chain by mid-March. Harvard Business Review.

Jalali, M. S., & Kaiser, J. P. (2018). Cybersecurity in hospitals: a systematic, organizational perspective. Journal of medical Internet research, 20(5), e10059. https://doi.org/10.2196/10059

Lezzi, M., Lazoi, M., & Corallo, A. (2018). Cybersecurity for Industry 4.0 in the current literature: A reference framework. Computers in Industry, 103, 97-110. https://doi.org/10.1016/j.compind.2018.09.004

Pendleton, M., Garcia-Lebron, R., Cho, J. H., & Xu, S. (2016). A survey on systems security metrics. ACM Computing Surveys (CSUR), 49(4), 1-35. https://doi.org/10.1145/3005714

www.ingramcontent.com/pod-product-compliance
Lightning Source LLC
LaVergne TN
LVHW052313200926
848481LV00002B/548
* 9 7 8 1 9 1 7 2 2 0 0 4 0 *